The Open University

Block 3

The Wars of the Three Kingdoms

Anne Laurence and Rachel C. Gibbons

This publication forms part of the Open University module A200 *Exploring History: Medieval to Modern 1400–1900*. Details of this and other Open University modules can be obtained from the Student Registration and Enquiry Service, The Open University, PO Box 197, Milton Keynes MK7 6BJ, United Kingdom (tel. +44 (0)845 300 60 90; email general-enquiries@ open.ac.uk).

Alternatively, you may visit the Open University website at www.open.ac.uk where you can learn more about the wide range of modules and packs offered at all levels by The Open University.

To purchase a selection of Open University materials visit www.ouw.co.uk, or contact Open University Worldwide, Walton Hall, Milton Keynes MK7 6AA, United Kingdom for a brochure (tel. +44 (0)1908 858793; fax +44 (0)1908 858787; email ouw-customer-services@open.ac.uk).

The Open University
Walton Hall
Milton Keynes
MK7 6AA

First published 2007

Second edition 2011

Copyright © 2007, 2011 The Open University

Edited and designed by The Open University.

Printed and bound in the United Kingdom by Bell & Bain Ltd, Glasgow

ISBN 978 1 8487 3910 9

2.1

CONTENTS

WHAT YOU NEED TO STUDY THIS BLOCK

- Units 9–12
- *Module Companion*
- *Visual Sources Book*
- Set book: Wallace, P.G. (2004) *The Long European Reformation: Religion, Political Conflict and the Search for Conformity, 1350–1750*, London, Palgrave Macmillan
- Anthology: Gibbons, R.C. (ed.) (2007) *Exploring History 1400–1900: An Anthology of Primary Sources*, Manchester, Manchester University Press/ Milton Keynes, The Open University
- A200 website
- TMA 03

Learning outcomes

When you have finished this block, you should be able to:

- understand the causes, course and consequences of the Wars of the Three Kingdoms (of which the English Civil Wars were a significant part) and the relations between England and Wales, Scotland and Ireland

- understand the history of the period in relation to the three themes of the course

- work more confidently with primary sources, both in the Anthology and online, and write an essay based on your use of sources

- work more confidently with secondary sources, using the OU library's electronic journals and other reference sources

- understand historians' debates about the Wars of the Three Kingdoms

- understand how historians use statistics.

Anne Laurence and Rachel C. Gibbons

INTRODUCTION

This block is about the Civil Wars that divided the peoples of the British Isles in the seventeenth century. It builds on the subject matter and skills of the first two blocks of the module, as well as your work on the themes. The religious divisions of the Reformation were still causing passionate splits; the nature of the state was in flux; and relations between England and the other nations that made up the British Isles on the one hand and the rest of Europe on the other were affected both by confessional (religious) divisions and by dynastic and economic considerations, many of which originated in earlier centuries.

You may well have a strong sense already of the drama of the English Civil Wars, when parliament took on the king – the clash between Roundheads and Cavaliers, the trial and execution of Charles I, the future Charles II hiding in an oak tree before fleeing into exile, Oliver Cromwell as lord protector, Puritans closing theatres and abolishing Christmas festivities, and the great battles of Edgehill, Naseby and Marston Moor (see the Block 3 chronology on the A200 website). It is the military aspects of the wars that are the most publicised in television programmes about the history of the period and through living history events and re-enactments by groups such as the English Civil War Society and the Sealed Knot. If you grew up in Scotland or Ireland, Northern or Southern, the seventeenth-century history you will have learnt will have had quite a different emphasis.

Differences in narrative history and traditions in each country reflect distinct experiences and preoccupations during this turbulent period. In the seventeenth century, the Isles of Great Britain and Ireland were ruled by the same monarch, but were not a single kingdom. All the Stuart monarchs until 1707 were separately rulers of the Three Kingdoms of England and Wales, Scotland and Ireland. The thirteenth-century conquest of Wales by England had been formalised by an Act of Union in 1536, absorbing the principality within the English kingdom. In 1541, the king of England had been declared king of Ireland, although the latter remained a separate sovereign kingdom. Therefore, in 1603, on the death of Elizabeth I, her successor, James VI of Scotland, became King James I of England and Ireland as well. This accumulation of titles and territories enhanced the king's power and prestige at the head of a far larger power base in Europe, but the three kingdoms did not create a single state, except to the extent that the foreign policies and general interests of the largest, wealthiest and most populous kingdom (England) tended to predominate and furnish the royal seat of residence. The one king held three separate crowns and, although his powers were similar in each kingdom, they were not identical and were conducted through separate institutions. If you think back to Block 1, Unit 2, the establishment of the Dual Monarchy of

England and France was intended to operate in a similar fashion. Henry VI was at one and the same time recognised as king of England and king of France in 1422, but each kingdom retained its own law courts, representative assemblies and national identity.

The individual relationships that needed to be negotiated between Charles I (*1625–49) and three different sets of subjects are reflected in the patchwork of conflicts making up the Civil Wars in the seventeenth century. There were two distinct phases of civil war in England (in the second of which much of the important action took place in Wales and Scotland). There were also wars in Ireland and in Scotland, where the issues were far removed from the central relationship between Charles I, the Church of England and the Westminster parliament, but nevertheless concerned the nature of the state, the status of adherents of different religious confessions, and the economic opportunities and restraints that governed people's behaviour. Each of the three thematic strands of A200, then – state formation, beliefs and ideologies, and producers and consumers – have a part to play in this block in terms of the causes of the Civil Wars, their impact and ramifications. As in Blocks 1 and 2, developments under the umbrellas of the three themes are often closely intertwined, as will be discussed further later in the unit.

SOURCES AND SKILLS

This block builds on the skills of Blocks 1 and 2. You will develop your abilities in reading primary sources to analyse the content and read critically. Even for those citizens who never fought or witnessed the battlefield, the experience of civil war might suffuse everyday life – and sources reflect that. Testimonies of personal experiences sit alongside widely disseminated accounts of events in news-sheets, and the printed and visual propaganda of atrocities intended to enrage and/or terrify. The skills of assessing bias that you practised in Block 1, when studying the English conquest of France, and in Block 2, with the conflicts of the European Reformations, will be put to good use here. You will also be introduced to statistical primary sources. The seventeenth century was a great age for information gathering by central and regional officials, albeit in what seems an irregular fashion by today's standards. The parish was the smallest unit of local government as well as of church administration so, when information was required on numbers attending Church of England services (a requirement by law for much of this period), how many householders were wealthy enough to pay taxes or how many men were eligible for military service, churchwardens would collect that information. Their findings do not always appear in neat tables: they were often in abbreviated or incomplete lists, or even narratives, from which historians need to extract data, count and compile results. In Unit 12, you will undertake an exercise with statistical findings that, as well as providing additional primary sources with which to analyse this period, will be good preparation for more detailed work in economic history methods in later blocks.

HISTORIANS OF THE CIVIL WARS

In terms of secondary material, you will continue to use Wallace in this block along with material accessed via the A200 website. You will see, too, how debates around a subject can develop among historians over time. The Civil Wars had hardly ended before histories about them began to be produced, offering different explanations and interpretations of events, often by those who had actively participated in them or were affected by their outcomes. Controversies have continued in the centuries since. In addition to historians' differing interpretation of primary sources, their assessments of each others' work, diverse standpoints and changing priorities can expand or redirect the field of enquiry in a controversial subject like the Wars of the Three Kingdoms.

EXERCISE

What factors might cause historians to revisit the history of the Civil Wars? Jot down some reasons.

Spend about 10 minutes on this exercise.

SPECIMEN ANSWER

Three possible reasons are:

1   The discovery of new materials from the period might alter our view of some event, development or interpretation.

2   Historians may disagree over the significance of certain events or developments, or over the interpretation of documents.

3   New questions arise, often as a result of contemporary concerns.

You may be surprised to learn that new manuscript discoveries are not unknown and are even made in well-known collections. A case in point occurred in 1970. An edition of the memoirs of Edmund Ludlow, one of the signatories to Charles I's death warrant, had been published in 1698–99, when there was some revival of interest in republicanism during the reign of William III (*1688–1702). This printed edition formed the basis of the edition published in 1894 by Charles Firth, a leading historian of the Civil Wars; the manuscript had by now disappeared. In 1970, Blair Worden discovered that a manuscript in the Bodleian Library in Oxford (which holds one of the most important collections of seventeenth-century manuscripts in the country) was a text of part of Ludlow's memoirs before they had been edited for publication in the 1690s. Perhaps Worden's most important discovery was that publication of the memoirs was clearly designed to contribute to the politics of the 1690s as well as adding to the history of the Civil War period (Ludlow, 1978, p. viii).

Rushworth and Nalson

In this section, we will examine two of the very earliest accounts of the wars. John Rushworth (1612?–1690) was close to the centre of events during the Civil Wars and first published a history in 1659 (the year before the restoration of the monarchy). A later reprint of his *Historical Collections* seems to have appeared in the 1670s in response to contemporary concerns about popery and arbitrary government. The second part did not appear until the 1680s, by which time an account of the civil war by a prominent parliamentarian was rather less controversial. In the early 1680s, however, an Anglican clergyman, journalist and ardent royalist, John Nalson (1638?–86), published an account of the origins of the civil war, explicitly trying to discredit Rushworth's work. If you have time, you might like to find out more about these two writers' lives from their entries in the *Oxford Dictionary of National Biography* (a link is available on the A200 website).

EXERCISE

Read Anthology Document 3.1, 'Writing the history of the English civil war: John Rushworth'. How does Rushworth justify the veracity of this account?

Spend about 20 minutes on this exercise.

SPECIMEN ANSWER

Rushworth tells us that he had early begun to collect historical materials and was an 'eye- and ear-witness' to many of the events he described, both public debates in parliament and private transactions of the Council of War.

DISCUSSION

Note how Rushworth is at pains to explain his historical method: 'a bare narrative of facts', 'not interposing my own opinion', using verbatim accounts and seeking verification of disputed points.

EXERCISE

Read Anthology Document 3.2, 'Rewriting the history of the civil war: John Nalson' (see also Figure 9.1).

1   How does Nalson characterise his method?

2   What faults does he find with Rushworth's work?

Spend about 20 minutes on this exercise.

SPECIMEN ANSWER

1   Nalson admits to not having 'tied myself strictly to the rules of a bare collector', but has tried to provide the 'circumstances, causes and consequences' of the materials he presents. He champions history that moves beyond the 'bare tale' of a narrative, but provides the 'long story' of background and reflection.

2   In promoting his own method in citing the 'real grounds, causes and occasions' of events and documents, Nalson implies that previous histories before (including Rushworth's) did not. He argues that Rushworth, having 'been an actor upon the stage', could not do anything but justify the parliamentary cause, and that his work is factually skewed by his desire to seek the favour of Richard Cromwell. However, he professes to be concerned not to sully the reputation of a man he doesn't know.

The examples of Rushworth and Nalson show how historians of different generations come to their subject with different concerns. The questions that most concerned Rushworth, writing under the government of Richard Cromwell and its collapse, were not those in the forefront of Nalson's mind in the later years of Charles II's reign. Nalson, a generation younger, was more

Figure 9.1   Frontispiece to John Nalson, *An Impartial Collection of the Great Affairs of State from the beginning of the Scotch Rebellion in the Year 1639 to the Murther of King Charles ... wherein ... the whole series of the late troubles in England, Scotland, & Ireland are faithfully represented*, London, 2 vols, 1682, 1683. Photo: The British Library. A beam from the divine eye rests on the figure of Britannia and an arm of divine justice bearing a flaming sword comes out of the heavens above a battle scene. A church behind Britannia burns, while the insignia of monarchy and episcopacy lie on the ground beside her and she is overlooked by the figure of a Catholic priest trampling the bible, with a horned devil behind his shoulder

concerned with the politics of the 1680s than with recounting the experience of the war.

Woolrych

Let us move to an article by a well-known historian of the seventeenth century: Austin Woolrych (1918–2004). In 2002, Woolrych published a magisterial narrative history, presenting a straightforward account of the events of the Civil Wars without giving much attention to historical method and theory. In this essay, written shortly after, he reflects on his writing experience and reviews historiography on the wars.

EXERCISE

Now read Austin Woolrych, 'Shifting perspectives on the Great Rebellion', in the Block 3 secondary sources on the A200 website. (You can choose to download and print out the article in PDF format if you prefer to read from paper rather than the screen. You will be using the article again in Unit 10.)

Woolrych was much respected for his histories of the debates in the army during the crucial revolutionary years of 1647–48 and of Barebone's parliament of 1653. In 2002, he published his book *Britain in Revolution 1625–1660* and, in this article, reflects on the experience.

1   From what position did Woolrych himself write?

2   How does he define 'historical materialism'?

3   What does Woolrych identify as the greatest collective contribution to the history of the Civil Wars?

4   What is the role of narrative history?

5   What was the position of Civil War history at the time that Woolrych was writing (2002)?

Spend about 30 minutes on this exercise.

SPECIMEN ANSWER

1   Woolrych writes of his own military experience, and his references to the Second World War and its aftermath suggest that this was a formative period in his intellectual development.

2   Woolrych defines 'historical materialism' as a theory explaining historical change through 'forces of production' (i.e. economic interests). In the case of seventeenth-century England, it meant a belief that the power of the aristocracy was contested by merchants and gentry whose economic power was not matched by political influence. However, he specifically situates the prevalence of arguments about the rise of the gentry (one of the main debates among early modern historians) in those historians' own twentieth-century world, when Marxist interpretations of history were prevalent.

3   The numerous local studies, which were of great importance for adding subtlety to our understanding of allegiance in the Civil Wars and of the wars' impact on lower levels of society.

4   Woolrych writes with admiration of the work of C.V. Wedgwood (1910–1997), whose books vividly tell the story of the Civil Wars but without venturing into much in the way of analysis or explanation. However, as Woolrych points out,

understanding precisely what happened is the key to explaining it – and his pleasure in this kind of writing (he was a fine stylist) is evident in his concluding paragraph.

5   Woolrych suggests that, at the time he was writing, historians' concerns about long-term structural change had receded and that a greater role was being afforded to 'human choice and human error, and to sheer contingency'.

DISCUSSION

As a soldier who had gone to university to study history under arrangements for demobbed servicemen at the end of the Second World War, Woolrych was particularly conscious of the military history of the Civil Wars. His earliest work was in this field and he maintained an interest in the military aspects during the 1960s and 1970s, when other historians, inspired by student protests and anti-Vietnam War demonstrations, on the one hand, and by the development of 'history from below', on the other, began to take a close interest in the revolutionary sects and political movements of the seventeenth century. The approaches and methods of Woolrych, and those of the historians he describes, to the seventeenth century were influenced by their own experiences and contemporary events.

When Woolrych writes of local studies of the Civil Wars, he is referring to a body of work influenced much more by 'history from below' than by devotion to particular localities. For many historians, a regional study has been a way of looking at how the larger events and developments of the war played themselves out in a specific local context. Their frame of reference is national developments against which local struggles were measured. A balance between local case studies and broader histories, focusing on change over time, is needed to construct the fullest picture.

The 'new British History': England, Scotland, Ireland and Wales

If you had been studying this period at a university based in England before the 1980s, the title most probably used would have been 'the English Civil War'. However, as I have already mentioned, civil conflict was not one war and not only fought in England. There were two wars on English soil – the First Civil War (1642–46) and the Second Civil War (1647–48). In the first of these, the Scots were allied with the Westminster parliament and in the second they supported the king. These campaigns were also part of a series of wars that took place all over Great Britain between Scots and English and between Scots and Scots, while in Ireland conflict involved different and shifting alliances between different groups of Irish, as well as Scots and English. The wars that took place in each of the three kingdoms of England, Scotland and Ireland cannot be viewed in isolation from each other, so it is important to study them together and to keep in mind the links between them. It is customary now among historians to refer to them as the Wars of the Three Kingdoms as a means of making that point clear. The chronology demonstrates how events fit together.

Woolrych refers to the impact of studies of Scotland and Ireland in changing our view of the wars. This change of emphasis owes something to the growing importance of regional identities within the United Kingdom since devolution and the creation of national parliaments and assemblies in Edinburgh, Cardiff and Stormont. Probably the most important point, however, is that there has been a reaction against monocausal explanations for the outbreak of the English Civil Wars. This is in part because historians gradually realised that the wars in England and Wales were inseparable from the contemporary upheavals in Scotland and Ireland. The study of these conflicts as 'Wars of the Three Kingdoms' is sometimes referred to as 'the new British history' – a description inspired by an article by a New Zealander, J.G.A. Pocock, in 1975, who argued that:

> 'the First Civil War' is a purely English term, appropriate only to English conditions – since in Scotland there was never a civil war, even Montrose [the Scottish royalist general] succeeding in launching no more than a Highland raid of a desperately unusual character, and since Ireland had not attained the degree of political integration necessary if the term 'civil war' is to have any meaning. The War of the Three Kingdoms was in fact three wars, originating independently if interconnectedly and differing in political character – a national rebellion in Scotland south and east of the Highlands, a frontier rebellion in the multicultural conflict zone of Ireland, and a civil war in the highly integrated political society of England – and flowing together to form a single series but not a single phenomenon.
>
> (Pocock, 1975, p. 605).

Pocock's ideas were particularly developed by Conrad Russell (1937–2005), starting with an article of 1987 in which he identified two common factors uniting the armed struggles in all three kingdoms: first, the three were all ruled by Charles I and, second, they were part of 'a multiple monarchy' similar in some ways to the federated lands of the dukes of Burgundy that you read about in Block 1. In other European multiple kingdoms, differences of religion between monarch and subjects had led to conflict, especially if the monarch had imposed, or was likely to try to impose, religious uniformity, as in, for example, the Dutch revolt against Spanish rule in Unit 7. Many historians would argue that confessional difference 'accounted for almost all the difficulties between the kingdoms of Britain between 1637 and 1642, and it caused enough trouble to leave very little room for any other [issue]'(Russell, 1987, p. 398). We will consider parallels with European conflicts in the seventeenth century and the place of belief in the Wars of the Three Kingdoms in Unit 10.

Summary

Most historians of seventeenth-century England now accept that they must consider connections between the three kingdoms, or at least offer an explanation if they are not according Scotland and Ireland a major part in the narrative. Nevertheless, much of this writing is primarily a contribution to understanding of the English state using Scotland and Ireland for comparison. Historians of Scotland and Ireland take different starting points, and there is no consensus between them as to the significance of the relationship between the struggles within the three kingdoms.

THE STATE IN THE BRITISH ISLES IN THE SEVENTEENTH CENTURY

In the last part of this unit, you will explore the interrelationships between the three kingdoms ruled over by King Charles I and what was involved in the governance of a seventeenth-century state. Think back to the discussions about state formation in Block 1, where you learnt that the word 'state' might not have been used in its modern sense, of a self-contained political unit with extensive powers over the lives of its inhabitants. Even so, fifteenth-century France and England both had distinct identities as powerful kingdoms. Think back, too, to the elements of the state identified by Andrew Brown within Unit 3: the degree of sovereignty (i.e. independence from an external power) of a ruler; the degree to which territories were united internally (through geography, and the way in which they were governed); a sense of common identity among a territory's peoples. These criteria are useful, but they are of a rather different order from one another. For example, it is relatively easy to establish whether a territory is independent of any external power, but it is much more difficult to identify the extent of common identity, especially after the Reformation when the religious unity of western Christendom had vanished.

The sociologists John A. Hall and G. John Ikenberry tried to define a state by identifying a set of qualities it required:

- a set of institutions with its own personnel including the means of violence and coercion
- these being at the centre (metaphorically rather than literally) of a geographically defined territory
- the monopoly of rule-making within that territory;

while the medieval historian V.H. Galbraith considered the necessary functions of the state to be:

- financial
- judicial
- administrative, including security.

The qualities defined by Hall and Ikenberry, and the activities identified by Galbraith (both cited in Aylmer, 1990), provide us with two slightly diverse ways of looking at the state. The political historian Galbraith is concerned mainly with function (what the state is able to do), whereas Hall and Ikenberry, as sociologists, are more interested in the impact of these functions on wider society. You probably are not surprised that scholars from different academic disciplines have different priorities, and are asking distinct questions about the same historical issue. And both have something to teach us as historians. Applying sociological definitions to the past can assist in assessing this society, at this particular point in time, against others, in previous or later centuries, and help us to make comparisons over time in a more meaningful way. In a module such as A200, which seeks to trace developments over a long period of time, this can only be a useful exercise. You will now have the opportunity to use these typologies to examine the British Isles in the seventeenth century.

Table 9.1 shows schematically how England (with Wales), Scotland and Ireland were governed. There is no need to learn this by heart; it is provided for the purposes of comparison with what follows in the block and you will be asked to look back at it when you arrive at changes later in the century.

The table needs some explanation. Although (as you have learned) the king of England was simultaneously king of Scotland and king of Ireland, you will see that each kingdom had its own parliament – that is, a legislative assembly where supreme power was considered to rest with 'the king in parliament'. The Scottish parliament, a unicameral (single-chamber) assembly, was for much of its life 'an irregular and short-lived event which brought together the political leaders of the kingdom to grant taxation, pass new legislation and adjudicate on disputes between its members' (Brown, 1992, p. 13). The Irish parliament, organised in two Houses like England, had less independence. The essential point is that England did not govern Scotland and Ireland: all three nations had the same king but separate institutions of government. However, Scotland and Ireland did not have independent foreign policies. Official relationships with foreign states were conducted by ambassadors and envoys sent from the king of England. That said, the administrations of London, Edinburgh and Dublin had separate powers to raise armies.

England had a highly organised local government for the period, based on justices of the peace and parish officers (constables to maintain order, poor law officials to collect and distribute poor relief) and lords lieutenant for each county responsible for summoning the militia. These local government officers kept order, and also collected taxes. Things were less uniform in Scotland and Ireland. In Scotland, the central belt and lowlands had a close relationship with the Edinburgh administration and much local government was in the hands of the kirk sessions. In the Highlands, however, it was in the hands of local nobles and gentry who operated independent jurisdictions with many ancient rights and obligations, calling on tenants for labour service, for example. There was a similar situation in Ireland: Dublin administered the Pale, the region around the city, through the courts and through JPs, but, beyond the Pale, local noblemen exercised considerable powers over their tenants. In both Scotland and Ireland, the central administration had to exploit the independent powers of the local landlords because they lacked the means to provide their own administration.

Table 9.1 refers to the institutions of the state, but doesn't necessarily tell us everything we need to know about its functions. Unlike modern states, medieval and early modern rulers did not have a monopoly on levying taxes, for the church had considerable powers to tax everyone, primarily by means of the tithe (in Scotland teind), a levy of 10 per cent on produce or income. The church also maintained its own judiciary in the form of bishops' (consistory) courts in England and Ireland, and presbyteries in Scotland. But as the king was the secular head of the Protestant churches of all of his three kingdoms, he was also the fount of all justice, lay and ecclesiastical.

Table 9.1   Government of England (with Wales), Scotland and Ireland up to 1649

	England and Wales	Scotland	Ireland
Ruler	James I (*1603–25); Charles I (*1625–49), advised by a Privy Council of about 20 members.	James VI (*1567–1625); Charles I (*1625–49). In the king's absence, royal authority was represented by the Privy Council, whose members were increasingly lairds and lawyers, as well as nobles and bishops.	James I (*1603–25); Charles I (*1625–49). Royal authority represented by the lord or deputy lieutenant.
Legislature	Parliament meeting at Westminster consisting of House of Lords (hereditary peers from viscounts up and Anglican bishops) and House of Commons (1 member for each borough and 2 for each county; 24 MPs for Wales) elected by men owning freeholds worth more than 40 shillings (£2) in the countryside, and on a variety of different property qualifications in the boroughs. Sheriffs were the local officials responsible for overseeing elections. The right to call and dismiss parliament was the king's alone.	Parliament meeting in Edinburgh consisting of a single chamber of 43 Scottish peers, around 50 gentry, burgesses representing 54 burghs, 14 bishops plus officers of state. Shire commissioners (about 27) were elected annually from 40-shilling freeholders, but not in all shires. (The property qualification was lower in Scotland as a Scottish shilling was worth less than an English shilling.) Business was directed by the Committee of the Lords of the Articles. The Convention of Royal Burghs separately dealt with legislation affecting burghs.	Parliament meeting in Dublin consisting of House of Lords (99 peers in 1634 and 24 Church of Ireland bishops) and House of Commons (235 MPs). Representation increasingly favoured Protestant settlers but there was no objection to Catholics sitting in either house. In 1640, the lords were evenly divided between Protestants and Catholics; in the Commons, about a third of MPs were Catholic. Poynings' Law (1494) required that matters dealt with by the Irish parliament had to be approved by the Privy Council in England.
Judiciary	Judges were appointed by the king. Local legal officers (JPs/magistrates) were appointed by the local bench of magistrates on behalf of the king. Church courts summoned by bishops dealt with matters to do with religious conformity (adherence to any church other than the Church of England was illegal), church buildings, the clergy, payment of tithes, administration of wills and morality. Manorial courts dealt with matters of land allocations in some parts of the country.	The Court of Session dealt with property cases; the High Court of Justiciary dealt with criminal cases. A system of JPs on the English model had been introduced in 1609 but was not implemented, and much local justice in reality was in the hands of noble and gentry landlords with 'heritable' jurisdictions, as well as burgh courts and kirk sessions.	Common law courts and Chancery on the English model operated in the Pale (the area round Dublin) and in some other areas of English settlement. Boroughs had JPs on the English model but little of the rest of the English infrastructure existed. Early in the century, vestiges of ancient Irish law, practised by Brehons, lawgivers to the clan chiefs, survived.

Executive	Ministers and secretaries of state were appointed by the king. In the parishes, constables and overseers of the poor were appointed by the JPs to maintain order and collect and administer the poor rate.	There was a very small executive in Edinburgh controlled by the Scottish Privy Council. Local government took place through the burghs and in both town and country through kirk sessions.	The lord or deputy lieutenant in Dublin Castle maintained an administration.
Foreign policy	The right to declare war, make treaties, end war was the king's alone.	Scotland did not have the power to negotiate with foreign states independently.	Ireland did not have the power to negotiate with foreign states independently.
Defence	Lords lieutenant and deputy lieutenants, appointed by the monarch for each county, were responsible for raising militias in times of emergency. The only navy was that of England.	Troops were raised through landowners as feudal subordinates to the king. After 1639, the Covenanters used committees through the presbyteries to raise troops.	The lord/deputy lieutenant could raise troops as could the four presidents of the provinces of Ulster, Munster, Leinster and Connacht (whose powers were similar to those of a lord lieutenant in England). The oath of allegiance to the monarch could be waived to allow Catholics to serve as soldiers.
Taxation	Only parliament could vote taxes for the monarch, but at the beginning of a new reign they voted certain taxes for life.	Scotland was much less heavily taxed than England and Wales. Much taxation consisted still of forms of feudal dues. Occasional taxes were granted for specific purposes by parliament. There was no customs union with England.	The Dublin parliament granted the king subsidies. There was no customs union with England.
Church	The secular head of the Church of England was the monarch; its ecclesiastical head in England, the archbishop of Canterbury. The country was divided into dioceses administered by bishops with their own system of courts for trying moral offences and non-payment of tithes (the tax of 1/10 of income levied on all householders) Services were conducted according to the Book of Common Prayer and the church was regulated by Canons passed by Convocation – an assembly of clergy.	The secular head of the Church of Scotland was the monarch, with administration by bishops. Overall control of the kirk rested with the General Assembly of clergy and laity, called by the monarch in 1618 and 1638. Beneath this was a system of regional presbyteries and kirk sessions – assemblies of clergy and laity that ran the church down to parish level. Services were conducted according to the Book of Common Order. The Book of Common Discipline regulated the government of the kirk. There was a minority of Catholics, chiefly in the northern parts of the country.	The secular head of the Protestant Church of Ireland was the monarch. The church had a similar theology and organisation to the Church of England. Church of Ireland services were conducted according to the Book of Common Prayer. The church was regulated by Canons passed by the Irish Convocation. The majority of the population was Catholic. There were Catholic clergy in Ireland but no formal hierarchy of bishops. There was a substantial Scottish Presbyterian population, chiefly in Ulster.

EXERCISE

Look back at the criteria for a state as proposed by Galbraith and Hall and Ikenberry, and over the contents of Table 9.1. Which of these territories seems to meet the criteria for statehood?

Spend no more than 30 minutes on this exercise.

SPECIMEN ANSWER

England (with Wales) was certainly a sovereign state, with an independent ruler and the power to make peace and war, raise taxes, and coerce its citizens. Scotland could do most of these things, except make peace or war with foreign states; likewise Ireland.

England (with Wales) was united internally, with a common system of government and administration. To some extent, the governments in Edinburgh and Dublin had contracted to local nobilities the maintenance of order in areas most distant from the capitals. Governments in London, Edinburgh and Dublin all had financial, judicial and administrative powers, but only from London (i.e. from the administration of the king of England) could defence against foreign attack be organised. In all three kingdoms, there was an established Protestant Church that could be considered as an arm of the state.

So, it is reasonable to argue that Scotland and Ireland had many, but not all, criteria of an independent state, but that England (with Wales) was certainly a state.

DISCUSSION

There are refinements that we might offer to the bare facts taken from the table. Scotland and Ireland had their own institutions and powers of coercion (through the judiciary and local officials). Both kingdoms' administrations had a monopoly on rule-making (allowing the church to be considered with the state). Their administrations had the power to raise military forces and controlled geographically defined territories, though that control was somewhat looser at the outer margins and, in all circumstances, existence of systems of government did not necessarily mean 100 per cent compliance with those systems. None of the Scottish or Irish administrative bodies were supervised by England, but they had to be carried out with reference to English interests: for example, Poynings Law (1494) required that matters dealt with by the Irish parliament had to be approved by the Privy Council in England.

THEMES

As this exercise makes clear, state formation is a central theme of this block – with particular reference to the nature of the dominant kingdom of England within the amalgamated territories ruled by the Stuart monarchs, and the ways in which the pressure of the Civil Wars challenged and altered political institutions. We shall look at producers and consumers by examining the economic triggers to conflict through royal demands for taxation, and in the context of a development of a war economy in England (where most armies were raised). We shall also discover how provisioning the war had considerable economic effects, as well as investigating the socio-economic impact of war on citizens.

The impact of beliefs and ideologies, whether religious or political, will be apparent, given that this block begins in an era when loyalty to the state/

political community was considered to be coterminous with membership of a particular confession. To prefer any other form of worship to that of the religion of the state and/or its ruler was effectively to hold treasonous beliefs. However, across the three kingdoms, there were sharp divisions over matters of doctrine and practice within the established churches, as well as between the established churches and communities worshipping outside them. England and Wales were predominantly Protestant, with small and infrequently persecuted Catholic minorities. Scotland's Catholic minority was larger, proportionately, and settled largely in the Highlands. Here, where at least half the population of Scotland lived, Gaelic was the dominant language. The Church of Scotland had a more Calvinist theology than the Church of England and, while it had bishops, the most important administration of the church was through a hierarchy of assemblies, culminating in the General Assembly of the Kirk.

Matters were rather more complicated in Ireland. There were three communities there, each of which regarded itself as culturally distinct. There were the Gaelic Irish – Catholic, Gaelic-speaking, with a clan-based society cut into by Henry VIII's land reforms. There were the descendants of the Anglo-Norman settlers of the twelfth century, mainly Catholic, sometimes Gaelic-speaking after centuries of settlement and intermarriage, but who regarded themselves as preservers of English language, law and custom. These 'Old English', as they were known, had traditionally been loyal supporters of the English crown against the native Irish, though since the Reformation they had been considered by the English government to be untrustworthy because of their religion. Finally, there were the 'New English and Scots', settlers who had come to Ireland since the mid-sixteenth century to take up land grants offered to Protestants from land confiscated from rebellious Catholic Irish families. In Ireland, beliefs and ideologies were closely tied to the theme of producers and consumers, in that access to the means of production (land) was often connected to religious affiliation.

CONCLUSION

The English state (embracing Wales) had all the institutions of a state, a sense of identity and a high degree of cultural integration. Alongside it were two nations whose claims to be states were ambiguous and which contained substantial populations who did not necessarily share their monarch's vision of the state. Differences in culture, tradition and belief between the three kingdoms would become more obvious and damaging as political tensions rose under Charles I.

REFERENCES

Aylmer, G.E. (1990) 'The peculiarities of the English state', *Journal of Historical Sociology*, vol. 3, pp. 91–108.

Brown, K.M. (1992) *Kingdom or Province? Scotland and the Regal Union, 1603–1715*, Basingstoke, Macmillan.

Ludlow, E. (1978) *A Voyce from the Watch Tower* (ed. A.B. Worden), Camden Society 4th series, 21, London, Royal Historical Society.

Pocock, J.G.A. (1975) 'British history: a plea for a new subject', *Journal of Modern History*, vol. 47, pp. 601–21.

Russell, C. (1987) 'The British problem and the English civil war', *History*, vol. 72, pp. 395–415.

Woolrych, A. (2002) *Britain in Revolution 1625–1660*, Oxford, Oxford University Press.

Anne Laurence and Rachel C. Gibbons

INTRODUCTION

In 1643, a year after the outbreak of civil war in England, the preacher Jeremiah Whittaker was one of many to note that 'these are days of shaking and this shaking is universal: the Palatinate, Bohemia, Germania, Catalonia, Portugal, Ireland, England' (quoted in Parker and Smith, 1978, p. 2). This was the period of the Thirty Years War (1618–48), which had broken out in Bohemia in 1618 with a revolt of Protestant subjects against a Catholic ruler, and would involve most European states at one time or another over the next three decades. In some respects, the Thirty Years War was a continuation of disputes you studied in Block 2, which had lingered on, changed shape and resumed, reinvigorated, at different times and in different places. We shall begin this unit by looking at the turbulence in Europe as a context for the wars that broke out in the British Isles, through:

- the situation in Europe in the early seventeenth century and England's relations with other European states
- historians' assessments of the relationship between developments on the continent and in the British Isles.

With that background, we shall move on to consider:

- developments in the British Isles that led to the outbreak of war
- debates between historians about the direct causes of the war
- a range of primary evidence of clashes within society, and the particular challenges that civil war posed to financial and administrative functions.

EUROPE IN THE SEVENTEENTH CENTURY

The Thirty Years War provides an important context for looking at conflict in these Isles, for Great Britain and Ireland were never isolated from the rest of Europe. Travel by sea was often easier than travel over land so, for example, residents of Kent could reach Calais far more quickly than Caernarfon, and, for traders from Edinburgh and Aberdeen, the Netherlands was a more convenient destination than London. Furthermore, each of the nations of the British Isles formed different relationships with other parts of Europe. While England, as the most powerful and wealthy kingdom, regarded Spain and France as dangerous Catholic powers and economic rivals, there were long-standing ties between Scotland and France and between Ireland and Spain. Trade with the Baltic had led to settlements of Scots in Scandinavia, while Irish and Scots mercenary soldiers fought all over the continent.

The Thirty Years War

EXERCISE

Read pp. 155–62 of the set book by Wallace. Read it rapidly, rather than taking detailed notes, and answer the following questions:

1   As what kind of war does Wallace characterise the Thirty Years War?

2   What part did England play in the war?

Spend about 20 minutes on this exercise.

SPECIMEN ANSWER

1   Wallace describes the war as waged for 'dynastic interest', motivated by 'political ambition' with 'religious overtones'. The account shows how there was a constant interplay between the great powers (Spain, the Habsburg empire and France) and a myriad of smaller states.

2   The Calvinist Count Palatine, Elector Frederick V, was the son-in-law of King James VI and I of Scotland and England. Because of this, in 1625 England joined a Protestant Union with Denmark, the Dutch Republic and Bethlen Gábor of Transylvania, and various imperial (German) states.

DISCUSSION

Note that the term used is 'England', for, as you recall from Unit 9, the *state* that negotiated with foreign powers was really that of England. The parliaments of Scotland and Ireland did not have independent foreign policies. MPs in the English House of Commons (Scotland and Ireland still had their own parliaments) implored both King James and his successor Charles I to join the Protestant coalition against the Catholic forces of the Habsburg emperor, and to send military assistance to the Protestant princes. But neither king showed much enthusiasm for military engagement in a continental war.

Soldiers from across the British Isles, though, served in most of the armies of continental Europe at one point or another during the Thirty Years War, with the Scots the most numerous. Both Alexander Leslie, commander of the Covenanting Scots army in the 1640s, and the marquis of Hamilton, a leading Scottish royalist, had served previously in the army of the king of Sweden. Owen Roe O'Neill, leader of the Catholic forces in Ireland in the 1640s, had served in the Spanish army, as had Murrough O'Brien, who served both king and Parliament during the Irish rebellion. Joseph Wagstaffe, a Warwickshire man who also fought for both parliament and the king during the 1640s, began his military career in the service of France.

You don't need to retain a detailed knowledge of the events of the Thirty Years War, but do need to have a sense of the extreme effect it had on every country in Europe, however peripheral. Figure 10.1 shows how extensive the war in Germany was, while Figure 10.2 shows the population losses for the period. Note how in those regions where over 66 per cent of the population was lost, there was a considerable concentration of battles. In areas such as the Rhineland, a good many of the losses must have been from armies passing through, destroying crops, livestock and commerce.

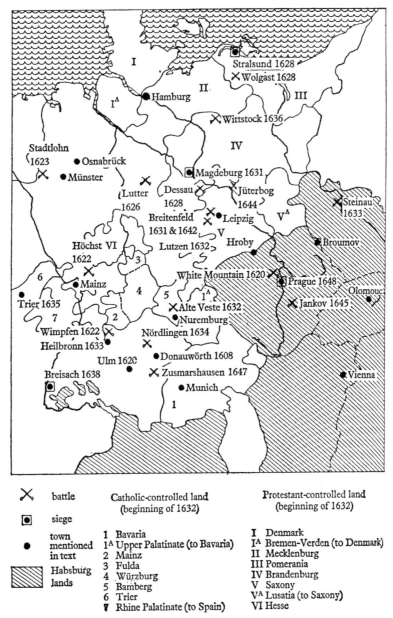

Figure 10.1   The Thirty Years War, from Geoffrey Parker, *Europe in Crisis 1598–1648*, Fontana History of Europe, 1979, Figure 8, p. 222

Frederick V (Wittelsbach) (1596–1632), Calvinist ruler of the rich Lower Palatinate on the Rhine and of the Upper Palatinate on the border of Bohemia, was the leading secular prince in Germany and one of those entitled to elect the emperor. In 1613, he married Elizabeth, daughter of James VI and I. In 1619, he was offered the throne of Bohemia, which led to the invasion of the country by imperial forces and Frederick's defeat and expulsion in 1620. By 1622, he had lost his German lands; he was formally deprived of these and his electoral title in 1623. He spent the rest of his life in exile. His sons Rupert and Maurice served in Charles I's army during the English Civil Wars.

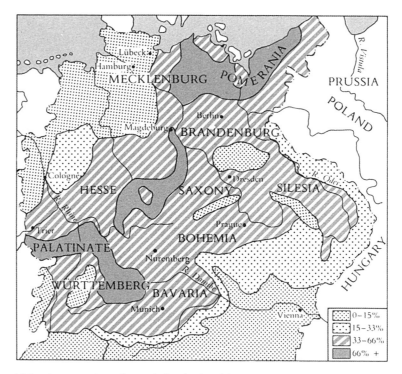

Figure 10.2   Germany: loss of population in the Thirty Years War, from D. H. Pennington, *Europe in the Seventeenth Century*, 2nd edn, London, Longman, 1989, Map 4, p. 587

A 'general crisis', states and confessions

That so much of Europe was, in the middle of the seventeenth century, taken up by war led historians to consider whether there was some connection between these struggles. In the 1950s and 1960s, a series of articles appeared looking for common themes in the causes and descriptions of these events. Some saw the 'general crisis' as inescapably linked with a fundamental change to the infrastructure of European economies, others saw it as a crisis of the state (Hobsbawm, 1974 [1954], p. 1; Trevor-Roper, 1974 [1959], p. 95). Although economic readings of the period are no longer as central to historical debate as they were in the mid twentieth century (as you saw when you read the article by Woolrych in Unit 9), such readings do inform the widely held view that the wars in western Europe were a series of connected events, even though they may not have shared a single cause.

At the centre of any discussion lie questions about the relationship between religious beliefs and state formation. Historians now debate whether the wars were the tail end of disputes that had started with the Reformation; that is to say, struggles concerned with trying to consolidate Protestant confessional states in the face of Catholic opposition. An alternative view suggests that religious issues were of less significance than the attempts of states to cast off late medieval feudal overlords (notably the Holy Roman Emperor) and to establish self-contained political entities analogous to modern states.

When a war lasts so long and involves so many different parties, the aims of the participants change over its course, and this complexity should be recognised. Inevitably there is no single 'correct' view, but the following paragraphs look at some of the central religious and political issues.

Religious self-determination was an important element for Calvinists, whose branch of Protestantism had not been recognised by the religious Peace of Augsburg (1555), and for Protestants ruled by Catholics. No one talked of toleration or multifaith societies in the early modern period, for allegiance to the state was defined by allegiance to the ruler, including his religion. However, few combatants went to war solely in the spirit of protecting their personal belief – dynastic and territorial ambitions provided important motives too. The individual German princes (the leaders of whom elected the Holy Roman Emperor from the Habsburg family) were suspicious of Habsburg ambitions and regarded each other as rivals for territorial power. The leader of the Protestant Union of Calvinist states, the Elector Frederick V, Count Palatine of the Rhine, jumped at expanding his territories (and gaining a crown) with the kingdom of Bohemia. His neighbour and rival, Maximilian I, duke of Bavaria, was a leading figure in the rival Catholic League of princes and was happy to accept status as an elector from the emperor for his service. The Lutheran King Christian IV of Denmark who, as duke of Holstein, was also an imperial prince, was more interested in territorial gains in the Baltic and Germany than in religion (Wallace, pp. 149–50, 157–8). Sandwiched between the Holy Roman Empire and the Ottoman territories, Bethlen Gábor, Calvinist ruler of Transylvania, turned out on a number of occasions on behalf of the Bohemian Protestants. On the Catholic side, Spain fought to support the empire, but also to protect its remaining territories in the Low Countries. There was little chance of it recovering control of the Dutch Republic, but the southern Spanish Netherlands (modern Belgium) were at risk, with enemies of the empire on all sides.

Two European states acted clearly from political interests rather than confessional ones, since they allied themselves *against* their co-religionists. In the early years, Elector John George of Saxony, a conservative Lutheran, stayed loyal to the emperor and, though he later changed sides to join his fellow Protestants, he was always a reluctant participant. Catholic France stood on the sidelines for many years, though offering subsidies to the Lutheran King Gustavus Adolphus of Sweden in 1631 and supporting the Protestant League of Heilbronn in 1633. Under Louis XIII and his chief minister, Cardinal Richelieu, France established itself as a worthy challenger to Spain and the empire, creating alliances with leaders who would support French territorial and hegemonic ambitions rather than sharing its religious confession in wars declared against Spain (1635) and the empire (1638).

Much of Europe experienced some economic decline with rising food prices in the early years of the seventeenth century. Producers and consumers were hit hard by the wartime devastation of trade, agriculture and manufacturing, and the dramatic fall in the population of many regions of Germany. Figure 10.2

shows the drop in numbers, some of which was as a result of peasants deserting their villages and the ruin of smaller landowners. The sheer extent of the war (as you saw in Figure 10.1) meant that, at one time or another, most regions of Germany and many parts of the surrounding states were ravaged by great armies and (often) larger trains of baggage and ancillary people, moving between arenas of conflict. Many soldiers were mercenaries, with scant interest in the dynastic claims of different German rulers, still less in their religious preoccupations.

This section should make it clear that, although, on the face of it, Europe was divided by confessional concerns, rulers preoccupied with territorial and dynastic gains might well set aside religious divisions.

EUROPE AND THE BRITISH ISLES

Although the English state was not much involved in the Thirty Years War, the reading public developed a taste for news; from the 1620s, weekly newsbooks, or *corantos*, published in Amsterdam and sometimes reprinted in London, provided news from the continent. There was an ardent audience for the succession of accounts of Catholic atrocities in Germany, many of them luridly illustrated to show the horror and barbarity of attacks against Protestants (see Figure 10.3). Several thousand Englishmen in total joined continental forces, in much the same way that Britons took part in the Spanish Civil War in the 1930s, and collections of money in parish churches and pious speeches in parliament offered help to refugees in Germany; however, no official military assistance was forthcoming. Other pamphlets produced for the English market dwelt on the miraculous deliveries, strange natural phenomena and portents to which events in Germany gave rise (Figure 10.4). This literature informed the responses of many men and women of the British Isles when civil war broke out at home. It inspired the more radical Protestant sects, who saw omens of the end of the world and biblical Last Judgement in the conflict, and confirmed the prejudices of mainstream Anglicans about the threat still posed by militant Catholicism – over fifty years after the Spanish Armada (1588) – to the survival of Protestant states.

The reasons why England played so little part in the Thirty Years War relate more to dynastic ambitions than they do to confessional concerns. Although the elector Palatine was James I's son-in-law and a fellow Calvinist, at the time of Frederick's move to Bohemia in 1619, James was trying to negotiate a marriage for his son Charles with a Spanish Infanta (princess) and wanted to do nothing that might disrupt the marriage prospects. Charles, as king, took some interest in his sister's fate and, in 1636, sent the earl of Arundel on an unsuccessful mission to persuade the emperor to restore the elector to his lands in the Palatinate.

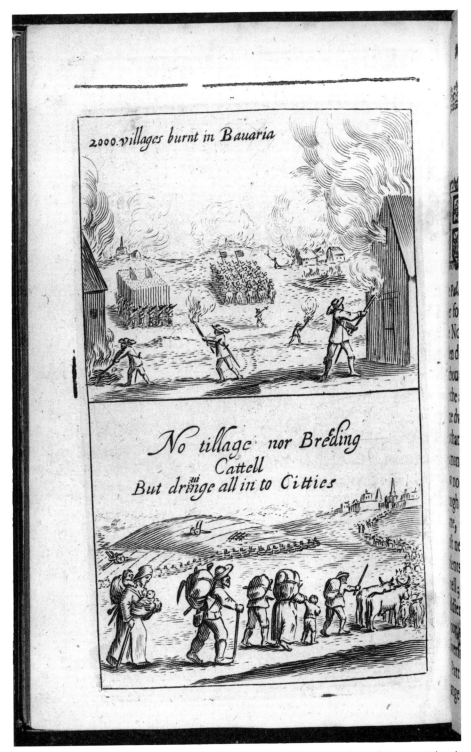

Figure 10.3   Illustration and page from Philip Vincent, *The Lamentations of Germany Wherein, as in a Glasse, we may behold her miserable condition, and read the woefull effects of sinne. Composed by Dr Vincent Theol. an eye-witnesse thereof; and illustrated by pictures, the more to affect the reader*, London. Printed by E. G[riffin] for John Rothwell, and are to be sold at the signe of the Sunne in St Pauls Churchyard, 1638, pp. 32–3. Photo: The British Library

miſerable eſtate of Germany.   33

CHAP. VII.
Of Burning and deſtroying.

FOr burning, pulling downe and rui-ning of Churches, Cities, Villages, the like hath not been heard. The *Swediſh* Army burned above 2000. Villages in *Bavaria,* in revenge of the *Palatine* cauſe : But their enemies ſpare nei-ther foes nor friends. What goodly houſes of the Nobility and Gentry, ſhall you there ſee fallen downe, or ſo defaced, as is ſcarce reparable without building new ? From what quarter ſoe-ver the army riſeth, they will be ſure to leave ſome dwellings in the aſhes, ſome in the ſmoake. To that paſſe it is now come, that every one that is a man, betaketh himſelfe to armes. There is now no other aboad, but ſome campe, no other Plough to follow, no other imployment but the warre, for hee that is not an actor with the reſt, muſt needes be a ſufferer among the miſerable patients. No tilling of the land, no breeding of cattell; for if they ſhould, the next yeere the ſouldiers devoure it. Better to ſit ſtill, than to labour, and let others reape the profits. Hence an univerſall deſolation.

Part of the people ſwarme as baniſhed in ſtrange countries, as I have obſerved in *Suiſſe,* at

Lauſan,

Figure 10.3   (continued)

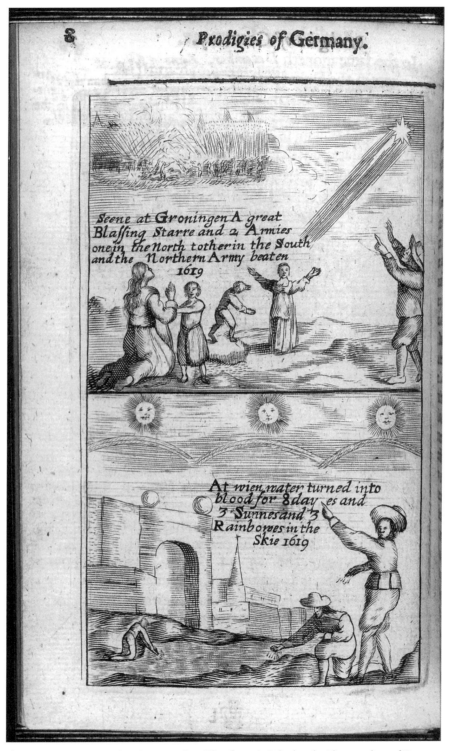

Figure 10.4   Scene at Groningen and at Wien from L. Brinckmair, *The warnings of Germany By wonderfull signes, and strange prodigies seene in divers parts of that country of Germany, betweene the yeare 1618 and 1638*, London. Printed by John Norton, for John Rothwell, and are to be sold at the signe of the Sunne in St Pauls Churchyard, 1638, pp. 8 and 9. Photo: The British Library

Prodigies of Germany.   9

In the same moneth *December*, *Anno* 1619. at *Groningen* in the Dukedome of *Brunswick*, appeared a great blazing Starre, and two Armies, one in the East, the other in the North, fighting against each other in the Heaven, so long till the Army of the North was slaine and defeated. This issued out, *Anno* 1626. the 25. of *August*, where few leagues from this place a fore battell was fought betwixt the King of *Denmark* and the Imperiall Generall *Tilly*, in which the King lost the field, and 4000. of his Army were slaine and taken prisoners: amongst them were also slaine 4. Danish Colonels, and a Landgrave of *Hessen*. Of the Imperialists lost their lives some 3. or 400. upon the place. We will not speak much of another conflict, which happened in the same Dukedome, when the fore-mentioned Starre was seen, where 500 were slaine upon the place neere *Calinberg*; nor of the bloody massacre, done by the Imperialists in the Citie of *Munden* in the said Dukedome, where 2500. Citizens and Souldiers were put to the sword most miserably by the Imperialists, the 27. of *August*, *Anno* 1626.

At *Wien* in *Austria*, the water in the Ditch was to bee seene like blood for the space of 8. dayes: likewise 3. Rainbowes appeared, and 3. Sunnes in the Heaven, in the beginning of *April. Anno.* 1619. here in the same place, and City, and in the same yeere, the 25. of *October* a great, and bloody fight was at the Donaw-bridge in the same Towne of *Wien*, betwixt the *Bohemians*, and Generall *Bucquoy*: in which encounter were slaine on the Imperiall side 4500. and of the *Bohemians* some 1000. and a great many wounded, which were

[margin: Two Armies fighting in the heavens.]

[margin: Three Rainbows and three Sunnes appearing in the heavens.]

Figure 10.4 (continued)

> **James VI and I** (1566–1625) succeeded to the throne of Scotland as King James VI in 1567, when his mother Mary Queen of Scots was forced to abdicate, and to the throne of England as King James I in 1603, succeeding Queen Elizabeth. He was brought up a Calvinist but believed fervently in bishops as an essential adjunct of royal power. He was succeeded in 1625 by his younger son Charles.

Historians, Europe and the Civil Wars in the three kingdoms

If England played so little part in continental affairs, why should we consider the two together at all?

EXERCISE

Turn again to Anthology Document 3.1, 'Writing the history of the English civil war: John Rushworth' that you read in the last unit. Look just at the second paragraph, beginning 'If you demand why my Collections commence so early ...'. What reason does Rushworth offer for starting his history in 1618?

Spend about 10 minutes on this exercise.

SPECIMEN ANSWER

Rushworth tells us his thought processes: he had considered starting in 1640 (the first meeting of parliament for eleven years) but then he realised that the events there depended on understanding 'some actions of the late king [Charles I] in dissolving four preceding parliaments'. Looking then at the reasons for the differences between king and parliament he found the origins went back to the reign of King James and 'the causes and grounds of the war in the Palatinate', and so resolved to start his history when the war there began.

Following Rushworth, many historians have looked to the continent for reasons for, or influences on, the breakdown of relations between King Charles I and his subjects in the three kingdoms. The most powerful thread connecting the arguments is religion. The Church of England, the reformed Protestant Church that had emerged from the Elizabethan settlement, was a recent creation, as you saw in Unit 8. The Anglican Church was less a unified system of belief and practice than an uneasy alliance of people with rather different ideas about what constituted a properly reformed church, who were united primarily by their allegiance to the king as head of the church and by their antipathy to the pope and to Catholic worship. To see Protestants in the Netherlands, Bohemia and the Palatinate come under sustained attack from united Catholic powers made English men and women feel profoundly vulnerable, especially knowing that in their midst were Catholics who, in 1570, had been instructed by papal bull that to murder their monarch would be a religious act. After the Gunpowder Plot had been foiled in 1605, the government used fears of Catholic terror plots and uprisings to justify a policy of fining Catholic worshippers and executing Catholic clergy and those who sheltered them. The Catholic minority in England was known to have links with hostile continental powers, and the presence of large numbers of Catholics in Ireland heightened fears of a Europe-wide Catholic conspiracy.

Under these circumstances, a king who favoured Catholics, as Charles I appeared to, seemed to many people in England to be committing a terrible betrayal.

This anti-Catholic sentiment was a profoundly significant force in English politics but why, between 1637 and 1642, did *all* nations of the British Isles rise in rebellion against the king?

EXERCISE

Re-read 'Elizabethan church settlement and civil war' in the set book by Wallace, pp. 133–9. (You read this in Unit 8.) Bearing in mind that Wallace's book is about the Reformation and its effects, how does he characterise the role of religion in the government of England and Scotland?

Spend about 20 minutes on this exercise.

SPECIMEN ANSWER

In England, Wallace identifies religion with royal rule, with the legitimation of the monarch, but he notes that Queen Elizabeth did, in fact, distinguish between her roles as head of state and as head of the church. He notes that religion provided the ideology for opposition to the monarch both from Catholics and from Puritans (those who believed that the church was insufficiently reformed), but that England avoided the religious wars that split such continental states as France by a policy of limited persecution of opponents of the national church settlement.

In Scotland, another form of compromise was arrived at, with different parts of Scotland accepting reformed religion to different extents.

In European politics, the Stuart monarchs' desire to be regarded as a significant power in Europe led them to eschew a strictly confessional foreign policy in favour of one that tried to curry favour with the leading European Catholic powers. This, combined with Charles I's attempts to reform both the Church of Scotland and the Church of England in directions that seemed to many ordinary subjects to smack of popery, produced articulate and well-organised opposition.

DISCUSSION

Wallace does not spell out why the relationship between the English kings and parliament was affected by the kings' desire for a pro-Habsburg foreign policy. The reason was that the monarch was dependent on parliamentary grants of taxation to govern in peacetime, even without the added expense of war. Parliament attempted to trade off its consent to taxation against the king modifying his foreign policy to support the cause of European Protestantism. And neither king would accept such a diminution of his powers to determine foreign policy and to make war and peace.

It is extremely difficult to separate religion both from foreign policy and from the ideology that legitimised the monarch's rule. As you have seen before in the module, state formation and beliefs and ideologies are thoroughly intertwined. James VI and I and Charles I believed not only that loyalty to the monarch (and thus to the state) was defined by adherence to a single set of religious precepts, but also that those religious precepts included the acceptance of the monarch as head of the church (instead of the pope) and that he was divinely ordained to hold that trust.

Historians have tried to address ideas about religion and England's position in the continent. John Morrill has suggested that 'The English civil war was not the first European revolution: it was the last of the Wars of Religion' (Morrill, 1993 [1984], p. 68). Morrill argues that, of all the discontents that the king's subjects in England nursed in the 1630s, *only* religion had the power to launch a war. He suggests we have been confused in seeking parallels between events in England in the 1640s and those on the continent, and that the English Civil Wars were not connected with the European wars of religion, but merely resembled them.

In contrast, Jonathan Scott argues that 'The crisis of 1618–48 threw not only the whole of religiously mixed, half-reformed central and western Europe into conflict, but Britain too, because Britain was part of religiously mixed, half-reformed central and western Europe' (Scott, 2000, p. 28). However, he also points out that 'England's troubles were unusual among Europe's wars of religion for being between, on the face of it, at least, not Protestantism and Catholicism, but contenders for control of the English reformation' (Scott, 2000, pp. 95–6).

Historians of Scotland and Ireland have also tried to examine the connections between the wars in those countries, religion and events on the continent. Maurice Lee argues that religion produced the ideological enthusiasm that was necessary in Scotland for successful opposition to the king's policies, though he believes, in contrast to Morrill, that it could not by itself 'galvanise enough of the people who mattered to produce a successful uprising'. He goes on to argue that 'the upheaval in Scotland was the work of the landed classes' who, in alliance with the kirk, could mount a successful challenge to the king which had nothing to do with ideas or events on the continent (Lee, 1984, p. 139). Tadhg Ó hAnnracháin makes the point that, in Ireland:

> the Wars of the Three Kingdoms took on their most European aspect because nowhere else in the archipelago had the forces of the counter-reformation established such a decisive presence ... in Ireland this reached a pitch closer to the continental experience because the distance between the competing religious positions was greater than in Britain.
>
> (Ó hAnnracháin, 2002, pp. 3–4)

EXERCISE

What common threads run through the arguments of these historians and how do they differ?

Spend about 10 minutes on this exercise.

SPECIMEN ANSWER

All of them accord religion a significant place. Morrill, Scott and Ó hAnnracháin all seem to take the view that it was religion that caused people to take up arms. Lee argues that (in the case of Scotland) it was an important element in raising opposition to the king, but that it could not alone have been responsible for armed revolt. His reference to 'the people who mattered' suggests that he believes that the support of this class was necessary for the opposition to succeed. Ó hAnnracháin observes that in Ireland, unlike anywhere else in the British Isles, divisions between

Roman Catholics played some part. For Scott and Ó hAnnracháin there was a direct connection between events on the continent and in the British Isles. Scott notes that elsewhere in Britain it was divisions between Protestants that led to war. For Morrill and Lee the connection between events in England and Scotland was superficial.

Summary

Early seventeenth-century Europe was riven by wars fought ostensibly over religion. In fact, these wars were not always about Catholic versus Protestant states/minority populations; they were more often fought to protect or extend territorial boundaries against political rivals and to extend the powers of ruling dynasties over their subjects. This interrelation between the themes of beliefs and ideologies and state formation is a pattern familiar to you by this stage of the module – and is one repeated in the Wars of the Three Kingdoms in the British Isles.

All of the historians discussed above highlight religion as a significant factor in the wars but, as we will discuss in the remainder of the unit, Charles I's personal beliefs about his rights and prerogatives as monarch (including the right to impose uniform religious practices) played a substantial part as well. Since we shall be dealing with a series of complex events across the three kingdoms, you will find it useful to keep the Block 3 chronology (on the A200 website) to hand from now on.

THINKING ABOUT CAUSES OF THE CIVIL WARS

On 22 August 1642, King Charles I raised the royal standard at Nottingham and effectively initiated war on his English subjects. This curiously archaic event, which was to feature as evidence in his trial (see Anthology Document 3.17, 'The trial of Charles I, 1649', part (b), 'Depositions taken against the king'), came as the culmination of a series of events and developing ideas that involved far more than the king's relations with the parliament at Westminster.

Identifying causes

Historians are in the habit of referring to 'pre-Civil War England' as if everyone in the 1630s knew what was about to happen. There were certainly signs that the relations between the king and a significant number of his most influential subjects had deteriorated. But to what extent did events of King Charles's reign and, in particular, the period 1629–40 when he governed without parliament – or, indeed, earlier developments – point inexorably to the breakdown of relations between ruler and ruled? Identifying the inevitability of civil war is not the same thing as identifying long-term causes, for how do we distinguish between a pre-existing event (i.e. something that simply happened to occur earlier) and a cause (i.e. something that materially contributed to a later event)?

We need to do an exercise in common sense. Here is a list of events that preceded Charles I raising his standard at Nottingham in 1642:

- 1536–39: dissolution of the religious houses (monasteries and nunneries) and appropriation of their property by the king
- 1558: accession of Queen Elizabeth to the throne of England
- 1588: defeat of the Spanish Armada
- 1603: accession of James VI of Scotland to the throne of England as King James I
- 1625: accession of Charles I.

Can we say that these events caused war to break out in 1642? To do this we have to explain *how* they did so. Let us take the example of the dissolution of the religious houses following the Reformation. Some historians have argued that, because this led to a free land market, the old monopoly of access to government by an aristocracy whose power arose from their territorial holdings was broken. Men who had done well as lawyers, civil servants and MPs acquired landed estates and were hungry for power. The consistent refusal of successive monarchs to give them political influence by offering them the prestigious offices that they felt their wealth and property warranted created a class of people disposed to challenge the monarch's powers. A religious policy with (arguably) economic undertones made a fundamental difference to the economic and political power balance in society, demonstrating again the interweaving of our three themes of beliefs and ideologies, producers and consumers, and state formation. Let us look more closely at what we would have to do to establish that the dissolution of the religious houses actually *was* a cause.

1 Note the time difference. Over 100 years elapsed between the dissolution and the outbreak of civil war, so the individuals who received the lands were long dead; possibly the great-grandchildren of the original recipients of the former monastic lands might be involved. So we need to establish whether the land market continued to be fluid or whether there was a flurry of activity for a period (it would be useful to establish what period) with the market then settling down.

2 What evidence is there that the increase in the amount of land for sale (which is incontrovertible) led to it being acquired by a different kind of person? In other words, how do we know that existing landowners did not simply use the market as a means of consolidating their already large land-holdings?

3 For what purpose did Henry VIII use the monastic lands? Was this a case of privatising a national asset for cash or services?

4 Were these new men excluded from office and were they aggrieved? And if so, did they continue to be aggrieved for eighty years?

The historian Lawrence Stone (1919–1999), one of the exponents of the idea that the causes of the Civil Wars lay in the distant past, believed that there was a shift of wealth away from church, crown and the old aristocracy and towards people he describes as 'upper middle and middle classes'. But he also argued that the rise of Puritanism and the spread of education encouraged the rising middle class to challenge the traditional wielders of power (Stone, 1972, pp. 75–6).

Looking at the rest of the list, it would be difficult to argue that Elizabeth's accession by itself could be the cause of a civil war eighty years later; it did have important consequences, though, particularly in guaranteeing a Protestant monarchy (a problem for Ireland). And Elizabeth's reign as a whole, once she proved to be childless, assured the union of crowns with Scotland since her heir was its Protestant king, James VI. The settlement that she agreed, when the church was re-Protestantised following the death of the Catholic Queen Mary, left much unfinished business for those members of the Church of England who believed that further reform in a Protestant direction was important. (This is dealt with briefly on pp. 133–5 of Wallace.) A good deal of this unfinished business surfaced under the pressure of Charles I's attempts to reform the church in what seemed to be a *less* Protestant direction.

We could make similar comments about the other events, but the important thing is that you can see that ascribing causes involves establishing a direct association between one event and another. That one event or idea precedes another does not necessarily create a causal connection. You need to explain *why* one thing caused another.

It is very much easier to see direct connections between events more closely related in time to the outbreak of war but merely being proximate in time still does not create a direct causal connection. So, if we want to say that the accession of Charles I in 1625 was a cause of civil war breaking out in 1642, we would need to explain *how* it contributed. In the next section we shall look at the events of Charles's reign and at their contribution to the breakdown of relations between the king and his subjects.

Charles I, second son of James VI of Scotland and I of England, was born in Scotland in 1600. His elder glamorous, learned and athletic brother, Henry, had died in 1612. James, anxious to cut a dash in European politics, wanted to negotiate a marriage for Charles, now the heir, with the king of Spain's daughter. When negotiations collapsed, Charles looked to France and, shortly after his accession to the throne in 1625, married Henrietta Maria, daughter of the French king, Henri IV. Her devout Catholicism and her strong influence over her husband led to suspicions that the king himself was moving towards Catholicism.

HOW DID RELATIONS BETWEEN THE KING AND HIS SUBJECTS BREAK DOWN?

Charles I and the eleven years' personal rule in England and Wales

Charles I succeeded as king on James I's death in 1625. James had resented parliament's demands for power over royal policy, but realised that he could not govern, even in peacetime, on the income he had. The monarch was expected to pay for the conduct of government from a variety of sources, which included both income from lands she or he held personally and taxes granted by parliament. So masques, mistresses, secretarial expenses, pensions for clients, bribes to foreign princes, wages for court officials and soldiers, the purchase of arms and equipment, and salaries for spies all came out of the same account. But James had learnt political skills during the difficult years when, as king of Scotland in place of his deposed mother Mary Stuart, Queen of Scots, he had had to negotiate with competing factions. Temperamentally, Charles was a very different character: inflexible, uncompromising, brooking no criticism, conscious of his dignity, decorous, uxorious, religious and a great collector of Renaissance art. Even his loyal subject Edward Hyde, the earl of Clarendon, said of him:

> His kingly virtues had some mixture and allay that hindered them from shining in full lustre, and from producing those fruits they should have been attended with ...

> He was very fearless in his person, but not enterprising; and had an excellent understanding, but was not confident enough of it; which made him oftentimes change his own opinion for a worse, and follow the advice of a man that did not judge so well as himself.
> (Clarendon, 1888, vol. 4, p. 490)

As king, he had three main concerns in England and Wales: how to fund his government, how to limit parliament's interference in his rule and how to reform the church. He showed remarkably little interest in his other two kingdoms, Scotland and Ireland.

Financing government

As was usual for a new monarch, Charles called a parliament, expecting that it would, as parliaments had previously done, grant him for life the income from tonnage and poundage (customs dues whose rate could be set by the monarch). His expenses were high. Apart from the usual costs of administration, he had funded an unsuccessful expedition to defend the Palatinate in 1625 and was committed to spending £20,000 a month supporting the Danes in the Thirty Years War. But parliament, fearful of his war strategy and unhappy about his proposal to take a Catholic wife, granted the king tonnage and poundage for one year only, though they also granted two subsidies (a form of direct tax, about £100,000). Customs dues (of which tonnage and poundage were a substantial part) typically formed about 30 per cent of government income. These sources of finance, together with the king's other revenues, came to far less than he needed to run the government in peacetime, let alone one which was engaged on foreign military ventures. Not content with his intervention in Germany, he allowed his favourite, the duke of Buckingham, to lead one expedition against Spain and another to support the French Protestant Huguenot rebels at La Rochelle, both of which were military disasters for the English.

So, from the earliest days of his reign, Charles was looking for ways to raise revenue. Each of the parliaments of 1625, 1626 and 1628 tried to exact concessions from him in exchange for grants of money, but he was utterly opposed to the idea of bargaining with his subjects. In 1629, he dissolved his third parliament and looked for alternative sources of income. In the ensuing eleven years without parliament he proved surprisingly successful by, as the historian John Kenyon put it, 'probing the wall of law and custom which protected his subjects' purses, hoping to find a gap through which he could press' (Kenyon, 1986 [1965], p. 52). In the absence of parliament, his subjects had to find other ways of expressing their opposition to his personal rule.

| EXERCISE | Look at Table 10.1. The left-hand column lists the king's chief revenue-raising activities. The right-hand column lists challenges to the king. |

1   What common features do you notice about the sources of revenue?

2   How did the king's subjects challenge his policies?

Spend about 15 minutes on this exercise.

Table 10.1   Sources of revenue and challenges to them

Sources of royal revenue	Challenges
Forced loans	
A medieval device, used by both Elizabeth and James I, whereby the monarch could solicit loans from the general public in case of threat. It was understood that there was no real prospect of repayment. Charles ordered one in 1626 (which raised £243,000).	In 1626, the legality of forced loans was challenged by judges. In 1627, large numbers of gentlemen refused to subscribe, were summoned to London and imprisoned. In the 'five knights case', five of them demanded that judges adjudicate the legality of their detention (not of the loan). The judges decided for the king by a narrow margin.
Tonnage and poundage	
Granted to the king for 12 months in 1625, he continued to levy the tax. After 1641, all customs dues were controlled by parliament.	Richard Chambers, a merchant, refused to pay tonnage and poundage in 1629, claiming in court that 'the merchants are in no part of the world so screwed and wrung as in England' (Tawney, 1928, p. 74). He was fined £2,000 for scandalous words and committed to the Fleet prison, where he remained for six years.

Knighthood fines

In 1630, Charles revived a device dating from Henry III's reign under which owners of estates worth £40 a year or more had to present themselves at the coronation in 1625 to be knighted. Those who had not claimed it had to pay a fee. Abolished in 1641.

Of particular importance to county gentry, many of whom refused, some claiming they had not been worth £40 in 1625. Edward Stephens of Gloucestershire brought an action in the Court of Exchequer, arguing he had not been summoned in 1626. The court found for the king.

Forest laws

From 1634, attempts were made to revive the king's right to any land that had once been forest. In 1642, forest boundaries were defined, closing this source of revenue, but the laws were not repealed.

Of particular importance to families with larger landed estates, though much former royal forest was regarded as common land.

Monopolies

In 1632, the granting of a patent to a corporation for the manufacture of soap exploited a loophole in the 1624 Act abolishing the king's right to grant individuals the right to a commercial monopoly over a trade or manufacturing process. Monopolies encouraged domestic innovation, regulated trade and discouraged competition, but also provided the crown with revenue.

Outcry against the tax referred to 'popish soap'. Other monopolies were established on salt, coals and starch.

Wardship and purveyance

The Court of Wards administered the estates of heirs below the age of majority and could choose their marriage partners. From Elizabeth's time, wardships of wealthy children were sold. The court was abolished in 1646.
Purveyance was the right of the royal household to buy provisions at cost price, and was abolished in 1660.

Both exactions had been regarded as abuses from Queen Elizabeth's time.

Ship money

This tax had formerly been levied on maritime counties to provide defences in time of war or threat of war. Charles extended the levy to inland counties. Declared illegal in 1642.

Legal queries in 1635 and 1636 produced a judgement that the king was entitled to levy the tax. In 1637, John Hampden was prosecuted for debt for not paying ship money. The judges found 7:5 in favour of the king.

SPECIMEN ANSWER

1   They were all existing measures. The king did not introduce new taxes, but adapted ancient ways of raising revenue.

2   Without parliament sitting, the king's opponents had to use the law courts to challenge his policies, especially to contest his right to levy extra-parliamentary taxation.

DISCUSSION

This antiquarianism was quite self-conscious. Sir John Borough, keeper of the records in the Tower of London, was commissioned to research methods used by earlier monarchs to raise money. Many of the devices he came up with exploited rights that had long fallen into disuse. Michael Braddick describes them as, on the one hand, 'fiscal feudalism' (forest and knighthood fines, wardship, monopolies) – that is to say rights that derived from the king's historic position at the summit of the feudal system – and, on the other, prerogative taxes (ship money, purveyance, forced loans), the right to levy which arose as a consequence of the personal powers of the monarch (Braddick, 1996, pp. 72–88).

EXERCISE

Read Anthology Document 3.4, 'Resistance to ship money, 1639'. What do you notice about the people who refused to pay ship money in the parish of Harrow?

Spend about 10 minutes on this exercise.

SPECIMEN ANSWER

The poverty of some of those required to pay is striking – Mrs Miller had a single piece of cloth seized.

DISCUSSION

This document shows how widespread and violent the opposition to ship money could be. Forty people in a single parish seems a large number of objectors (though we do not know how large the parish was). It is striking how poor some of the tax-paying public was. Women could be householders (they were usually widows, occasionally spinsters) and were liable for taxes, but had none of the political rights of a householder.

John Hampden (1594–1643), a Buckinghamshire MP, in 1627 refused to pay a forced loan and in 1635 refused to pay ship money. A leading member of the Short and Long Parliaments, he was one of the five MPs the king attempted to arrest in 1642. He raised a regiment of foot for parliament in 1642 and was killed at the battle of Chalgrove.

While the objections of poorer people might have been an irritation to the king and his officials, a more significant challenge was mounted in the law courts when the former MP John Hampden refused to pay and was prosecuted for debt. Of twelve judges, seven found for the crown. One of the dissenting judges, Sir Robert Berkeley, extended his consideration far beyond the simple matter of a country gentleman's unpaid bill and used the occasion to declare that the king's subjects 'have a birthright in the laws of the kingdom. No new laws can be put upon them, none of their laws can be altered or abrogated, without common consent in parliament' (quoted in Kenyon, 1986 [1965], p. 100).

Cases challenging the king's right to levy extra-parliamentary taxation brought up such broad constitutional issues as the king's right to order a subject's imprisonment and the distinction between the king's ordinary and emergency powers. In turn this led to conflict between the king and the judiciary, and

Lord Justice Crew was dismissed in 1626 for refusing to admit the legality of the forced loan.

As well finding new sources of income, royal officials tried to make tax collection more efficient – a policy especially promoted under the name of 'the policy of thorough' by Charles's close allies the archbishop of Canterbury, William Laud, and the president of the Council of the North, Thomas Wentworth. 'Nowadays the uttermost that all his Majesty's ministers can do scarcely restrains the people within the bounds of respect and obedience' claimed Wentworth, setting himself the mission to reverse this (Sharpe, 1992, p. 135).

William Laud (1573–1645) was president of St John's College, Oxford, and vice-chancellor of the university. Appointed successively bishop of St David's, Bath and Wells, and London, he became archbishop of Canterbury in 1632. He wanted to make Anglican worship more reverential, to reinstate ceremony and to emphasise the sanctity of the sacraments. To improve the quality of the clergy, he tried to raise clerical incomes by recovering ecclesiastical property and revenues that had passed to lay people. He aspired to extend English forms of worship to Scotland. As one of the king's most influential advisers in the 1630s, he was impeached and executed in 1645.

Thomas Wentworth, earl of Strafford (1593–1641), a Yorkshire gentleman and MP, had been a leading opponent of the king's policies in the 1620s. Appointed lord president of the Council of the North by the king in 1628, he went to Ireland in 1633 as deputy lieutenant, where he tried to reform both the Church of Ireland and the government's finances. He was created earl of Strafford and promoted to lord lieutenant (a change of title rather than of role) in 1640. He was tried by parliament for his part in encouraging the king to use an army against his subjects and executed in 1641.

The unpopularity both of the fiscal devices used by the king and of his counsellors consolidated opposition to the king. Many of his subjects, forced now to use the law courts to challenge royal policy in the absence of parliament, began seriously to question whether a state in which all powers flowed from the king was sustainable.

The church

Apart from concerns about the propriety of the king governing without parliament and conducting a foreign policy allying him with the Catholic powers of Europe, his subjects harboured deep suspicions about his attitude to the Church of England, of which he was head. Many of them, clerical and lay, believed that the Elizabethan church settlement had not created a sufficiently

Protestant church, and that the Church of England was in urgent need of
reform. Attendance at church services was compulsory and non-attenders could
be fined; it was illegal to hold or attend services outside the church. Reformers
faced a king who believed that his kingship was derived from God, that
Anglican (Church of England) bishops were the direct spiritual descendants of
Christ's apostles, and that dissent from the beliefs and ceremonies of the
church amounted to treason. Even to question these beliefs and practices was
to arouse the king's displeasure, and there was a formidable array of devices at
his command to enforce conformity. In particular, there were the prerogative
courts of Star Chamber and High Commission, which were able to impose
severe penalties on dissidents such as William Prynne, Henry Burton and John
Bastwick who, in 1637, were branded with hot irons and had their ears
cropped for publishing pamphlets against the government of the church by
bishops (episcopacy). There was something noble about the men, and they
became popular heroes, but they were, in their own ways, just as unmoving as
the king.

If the king's subjects were unhappy with his religious views at the start of his
reign, his policies did nothing to win them over. In 1633, he appointed as
archbishop of Canterbury William Laud, who owed his rapid career
advancement to the king's confidence in him (see p. 138 of the set book by
Wallace). Laud, like the king, was not a convinced predestinarian; both men
inclined to the views of the Dutch theologian Jacob Arminius, who argued that
individual believers' salvation was not foreordained; this made his appointment
extremely controversial. But Laud's primary concern was with the decorous
conduct of religious services in surroundings that would inspire congregations
with the presence of God. As archbishop, he extended the programme of
rebuilding churches (many of which were in a considerable state of disrepair);
most noteworthy was the restoration of old St Paul's Cathedral (see Figure
10.5) under the direction of the king's surveyor, Inigo Jones. This concern with
the externals of worship convinced those who wanted reform in a more
Protestant direction that the king and his archbishop were leading the church in
the opposite direction, towards a form of Catholicism.

Laud himself believed that he was enforcing existing measures that had long
been flouted. The rules governing the church, the canons, last revised in 1604,
specified in some detail how churches were to be furnished and equipped.
Laud set about ensuring that every church conformed to the canons, and parish
officials were authorised to acquire missing items, such as prayer books or
coverings for the communion table. During the 1630s, he reported to the king,
for example, that 'the greatest part of Wiltshire [is] overgrown with the
humours of those men that do not conform' and that religious radicals in
Ashford, Kent 'put a great many simple people, especially women, into great
distemper against the church' (Laud, 1847–60, vol. 5, part 2, pp. 324, 347). To
carry out his reforms, however, the archbishop needed an effective episcopate.
He believed in the apostolic succession of bishops (that they were descended
by the laying on of hands in a continuous line from Christ's apostles) and the
spiritual authority that this descent conferred, but he also saw them as the

Figure 10.5   Wenceslaus Hollar, *Old St Paul's from the East after Restoration*. Photo: Guildhall Library, City of London

church's executive arm, through whom any changes might be effected and lax observance of existing regulations tightened up.

The real change came with Laud's injunctions of 1637. Since the early days of Elizabeth's reign, the communion table had been positioned in the centre of the chancel in such a way that communicants could gather round it (as you have seen at Hailes church on DVD 1). Instead, the injunctions now required that the communion table be removed to the upper end of the chancel, placed along the east wall, and railed off. Plate 10.2 in the *Visual Sources Book* shows the communion table (4) set against the east wall and raised up on steps, behind rails (5). The two positions represented fundamental differences of attitude to the place of the sacraments in Christian worship. For Puritans, following the practice of the Elizabethan church, the bread and the wine of the communion service *commemorated* Christ's last supper and were to be treated respectfully, but were to be taken communally as a symbol of Christ's role as saviour. For the king, Archbishop Laud and their supporters, the sacraments were to be revered, to be received by *kneeling* communicants before the altar representing Christ's sacrifice on the cross. This symbolic position may have horrified Puritans, but historians have recently begun to challenge whether Laud's reforms were as widely unpopular as previously thought. Fincham and Tyacke argue that many of the laity were drawn to 'the beauty of holiness' and contributed their own money to the purchase of vessels and adornment for their parish's communion table in the 1630s (Fincham and Tyacke, 2007, p. 267) – bequests that bear comparison with those of the late Middle Ages that you saw in Unit 4.

Laud used his powers as archbishop to try to secure uniformity of practice in the church. In particular, he used visitations, the periodic enquiries ordered by the archbishops, bishops and their subordinate archdeacons about what was going on each parish. The questions (articles of enquiry) were based on the Anglican canons, but each bishop interpreted the canons in his own way in a list of instructions, which (since the canons did not comprehensively lay down the law about every single aspect of church life) left a good deal of room for manoeuvre. The lay churchwardens of each parish were summoned by the archdeacon to answer the questions on behalf of the parish. On the face of it, these surveys seem to be rather limited, but they do provide us with a surprising amount of information about the activities of ordinary people.

EXERCISE

Turn now to Anthology Document 3.5, 'Episcopal visitation articles and returns of the 1630s', and look at extract (a). This is an extract from the 122 questions asked in the visitation of the parishes in the diocese of Hereford in 1635.

1　Looking at the headings (numbered 1–8) what do you notice about the range of activity encompassed?

2　Looking at the content of some of the sections, what can you tell about the relationship between church and state?

3　How might we use a document such as this to learn more about parish life?

Spend about 20 minutes on this exercise.

1   These questions are not just about worship, or even about religious belief: they are about the behaviour and morality of everyone in the parish. There are special questions about medical practitioners, schoolmasters and midwives (who had to be licensed by the bishop).

2   The two are very closely connected. In question 1.1, parishioners are required to observe the king's declaration about settling religious differences, and in question 4.9, the clergy are required to 'teach and declare the lawful authority which the king hath over the state, both ecclesiastical and civil'. The idea of loyalty to the state was inextricably tied up with subscribing to a single ecclesiastical regime.

3   The headings and the questions themselves tell us what the authorities (the archbishops and bishops appointed by the king) considered to be important and what matters they considered to be disruptive of society. They cannot tell us about the king's subjects' private beliefs.

By comparing questions from visitations over a period of years, we can discover how the authorities' priorities changed. Thinking back to Block 2, you might expect, for example, that a visitation taking place during the reign of Henry VIII would ask different questions about church furnishings from those asked by a visitation in Elizabeth's reign. Compare the details of the placing of the communion table ('conveniently') in 1635 (Anthology Document 3.5(a), question 3.2) with Bishop Wren's orders of 1636 (Anthology Document 3.5(b)) in which parishes were instructed to place the table 'close under the wall of the chancel'. And in 1638, the visitation articles (Anthology Document 3.5(c)) contain a direct question about whether the altar is at the east end and railed off. But, as well as details of furnishings, the articles implicitly tell us something about the state and its ideology: its theory of rule. In Anthology Document 3.5(a), question 4.9, 'the just abolishing of all foreign power' is a reference to the widely held belief that Roman Catholics owed allegiance to the papacy (a foreign ruler) rather than to the king of England.

> **Matthew Wren** (1585–1667) was bishop of Hereford (1634), bishop of Norwich (1635) and bishop of Ely (1638–67). A close associate of Archbishop Laud, he was an enthusiastic exponent of his church reforms and was much hated by the numerous Puritans in his two East Anglian dioceses. He was held in the Tower of London for much of the Civil Wars and Interregnum and returned to his diocese at the Restoration.

To understand life in the parishes (and remember that most people lived in small rural settlements and not in towns) we need the *answers* to the questions provided by the churchwardens.

Turn again to Anthology Document 3.5, 'Episcopal visitation articles and returns of the 1630s', and look at extract (d). The churchwardens of the parish of Shepreth were replying to the questions set out in Wren's visitation of 1638 (some of which are given in extract (c) – the other questions were very similar to those in extracts (a) and (b)).

1   What offences were noted?

2   How compliant was the parish to the requirements?

Spend about 10 minutes on this exercise.

1   One parishioner refused to pay the parish rate and another abused the minister.

2   The parishioners seem to have been most compliant and obedient to the requirements for baptism, marriage and taking Holy Communion, with an exemplary, politically loyal and conformist minister. The church had been rearranged with the communion table at the east end and steps up to it.

The performance of the parishioners might seem almost too good to be true: Bishop Wren was subsequently charged with employing clerks to fabricate visitation returns for his diocese, although very few actual returns survive. On the other hand, conformity to changing official demands may well just have been something that the quiet majority of parishioners accepted. 'Few wished to remain outside the Christian community' (Haigh, 2007, p. 77), so objections would have to be passionately held for a person to take a public stand.

The matters that these questions dealt with might nowadays seem to be of little significance, but, as you'll remember from your work in Unit 4, the furnishings of a church carried important doctrinal messages which the government used to display ecclesiastical changes in a manner evident to the meanest parishioner. The state actively used the beliefs of the church as a test of the loyalty of its subjects.

Summary

This section shows how Charles I managed to alienate many of his ordinary subjects and also those whom we might call members of the political nation – MPs and peers, and the kinds of men (for they were only men) who were local government officers, such as justices of the peace, sheriffs and members of urban corporations. The issues that most antagonised them were his attempts to raise money in ways not authorised by parliament and to introduce religious changes which seemed to represent a return to a religious regime that was associated in many people's minds with tyranny. But, resistant though the population was to both Charles's financial expedients and the religious changes, he managed to govern perfectly satisfactorily on the income he had, especially after the country was extricated from foreign military enterprises in 1628.

PERSONAL RULE OR TYRANNY 1629–40?

Historians have long debated the significance of the eleven years' personal rule, the period 1629 to 1640 when Charles ruled without parliament. Some take the view that this was a period of tyranny when Charles was fuelling fears about his absolutist ambitions and his popish religious policies. Others argue that his policies, however unpopular, are not sufficient to explain the outbreak of war in 1642. So what happened to turn a period of domestic peace into a civil war? Here we need to look beyond England.

Scotland, the prayer book and the bishops' wars

James VI had managed to make himself the most powerful king of Scotland since Robert the Bruce. He replaced the medieval idea of personal monarchy with the divine right of kings and bought the acquiescence of his more powerful subjects with grants of former church lands. James's accession to the English throne in 1603 did not diminish his power in Scotland, but Charles, succeeding to the throne in 1625, cared little for his northern kingdom and left its government to other bodies: the Privy Council in Edinburgh, comprising prominent laymen and lawyers and Scottish bishops (whose ecclesiastical powers were much less than those of English bishops); royal officials and judges; and the unicameral Scottish parliament (see Figure 10.6). In 1632 he had commissioned a new building to

Figure 10.6   James Gordon of Rothiemay/F. de Wit, *The Parliament House, Edinburgh* (designed by Sir James Murray of Killaberton), *c.*1646, engraving. Photo: Reproduced courtesy of the Royal Commission on the Ancient and Historical Monuments of Scotland

provide a permanent home for the Scottish parliament and for the court of session. The following year (1633), parliament met for the first time in Charles's reign when he visited the country for his coronation, which was the point at which he insisted that the English Book of Common Prayer be used instead of the Book of Common Order used in Scotland since the Reformation. He also asked the Scottish bishops to draw up a new liturgy based on that used in England.

Charles's desire, supported by Archbishop Laud, to impose greater religious uniformity between England and Scotland was prefigured in his father's attempts to give bishops in the Church of Scotland greater powers (there were no claims to apostolic succession as there were in England – bishops were seen as senior royal officials). The measure embodying this, the Five Articles of Perth (1618), required that the congregation receive the sacraments kneeling (we have already seen that this was a contentious matter in England), and was met with great opposition. A minister wrote in 1619 'every honest minister in all our east parts will rather leave their ministry or they yield one jot to the bishops' (Foster, 1975, p. 187). And the governing body of the Church of Scotland, the General Assembly of the Kirk, was given no opportunity to comment. In 1636, new church canons were published incorporating the Five Articles of Perth as well as elements of the English canons of 1604 and requiring the use of the liturgy still being composed by the Scottish bishops.

This new liturgy, published in 1637, was an amalgam of Scottish and English practice and was prefaced with a royal proclamation commanding its use. It provided for the communion table to be set altar-wise with its back to the east wall; the universal Scottish practice had been for communicants to sit on forms around the communion table and for communion to be administered no more than once a year after considerable preparation of fasting, sermons and examination of communicants. At its first major public airing, at St Giles Cathedral in Edinburgh on 23 July 1637, a riot broke out (see Figure 10.7). This was described by Henry Guthrie, a Church of Scotland minister:

> No sooner was the service begun, but a multitude of wives and serving women in the several churches, rose in a tumultuous way, and having prefaced awhile with despiteful [contemptuous] exclamations, threw the stools they sat on at the preachers and thereafter invaded them more nearly, and strove to pull them from their pulpits, whereby they had much ado to escape their hands, and retire to their houses. And for the bishop (against whom their wrath was most bent) the magistrates found difficulty enough to rescue him.
>
> (Fyfe, 1928, p. 137)

More significant was the large number of petitions against the new liturgy and against 'the pride and avarice of the prelates seeking to overrule the whole kingdom' (Donaldson, 1978 [1965], p. 311). There followed a period of riots and disturbances in Edinburgh interspersed with royal proclamations against the petitioners, while the Scottish Privy Council tried to maintain order despite popular demands for the removal of bishops from the council. In November 1637, the petitioners elected their own delegates and forced the Privy Council

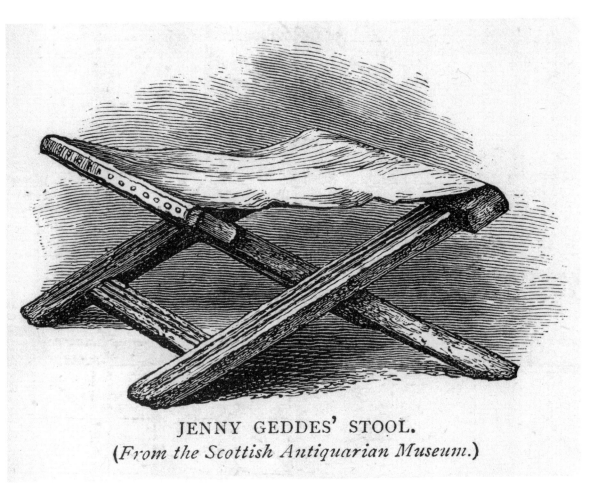

JENNY GEDDES' STOOL.
(From the Scottish Antiquarian Museum.)

Figure 10.7   *Jenny Geddes' Stool*, St Giles, 1882, engraving, from James Grant, *Cassell's Old and New Edinburgh*, vol. 1 London, Cassell, Petter, Galpin & Co., 1882, p. 146. Geddes, a poor market woman, allegedly initiated the stool throwing in St Giles's cathedral, but the first reference to her participation dates from 1670

to recognise them as a body with whom to negotiate. Popular protest and petitioning were the means by which an increasingly politically aware and motivated populace could voice their dissent, given that the electoral franchise was limited to men of property worth forty shillings per year, as it would remain into the nineteenth century (see Blocks 4 and 5).

> **Archibald Johnston of Wariston** (1611–1663) was a lawyer, clerk of the General Assembly of 1638, a leading Covenanter and judge. He rejected the Engagement between the Scots and the king of 1647 and reluctantly accepted office during the Cromwellian occupation of Scotland in the 1650s. After the restoration of Charles II in 1660, he was sentenced to death and hanged for his part in the opposition to the king.

Meanwhile, Alexander Henderson and Archibald Johnston of Wariston, respectively a minister and lawyer, drew up a National Covenant, which stated that changes in the church required the approval of the General Assembly of the Kirk and parliament, and could not simply be decreed by the king; it said nothing about what innovations were acceptable. In February 1638, residents of Edinburgh signed it; it was then circulated to every burgh and parish for subscription and note was taken of anyone who refused to sign. In response, the king appointed the marquis of Hamilton to negotiate with the Covenanters but only to allow a General Assembly of the Kirk and a meeting of parliament if the Covenant was repudiated. By this time most nobles and lawyers had signed the Covenant and had already started to make military preparations. In September 1638, the king agreed to revoke the new prayer book and canons and to call a General Assembly in Glasgow in November 1638, the first to meet since 1618. The General Assembly pronounced on both the prayer book and the canons.

| EXERCISE | Read Anthology Documents 3.6, 'The National Covenant, 1638', and 3.7, 'Acts of the General Assembly at Glasgow, 1638'. What differences do you notice between the two document extracts? |

Spend about 15 minutes on this exercise.

| SPECIMEN ANSWER | The extract from the Covenant is concerned with securing as wide agreement as possible that ecclesiastical innovations must be approved by 'free assemblies' and parliaments. It professes obedience to religion and the desire not to diminish the king's authority. The General Assembly, by contrast, not only condemned the innovations and those who promulgated them ['pretended prelates' refers to the bishops; 'pretended' here means so-called rather than false], but threatened penalties against anyone using the new prayer book, so abhorrent were the doctrines it contained. It asserted the supreme jurisdiction of the General Assembly over any changes in the Church of Scotland and simply abolished bishops. |

The radical steps taken by the General Assembly led to the marquis of Hamilton, the king's commissioner, trying to dissolve the meeting, but defiantly it sat on. Meanwhile, the Covenanters, who now included a number of aristocrats who had served in continental armies fighting the Thirty Years War, carried on arming. In March 1639, the king set forth for Scotland with an ill-equipped and poorly disciplined army, with the promise of troops to be sent from Ireland by Wentworth. Those Scots who had rallied to him (some of the Scottish nobility and many Highlanders, for example), rather than joining the Covenanters, had more success than the English forces, but not enough to prevent the English from being turned back at Berwick-on-Tweed by the Covenanting army under General Alexander Leslie. The truce made at Berwick to end this First Bishops' War required both sides to disband their armies while the king undertook to come to Scotland for meetings of parliament and the General Assembly of the Kirk.

Alexander Leslie (?1580–1661) had served with English forces in the Netherlands and as marshal in the Swedish forces in Germany. Returning to Scotland in August 1638, he led the Covenanting army in the First and Second Bishops' Wars, and the Scots army that joined the parliamentary forces in 1644. When the Scots declared for the king in 1647, Leslie (now Lord Leven) was relieved of his command. He reluctantly led a Scots army against Cromwell and was defeated at Dunbar (1650). He was held prisoner for a time in London, but was released and spent the rest of the Interregnum at home in Fife.

It soon became apparent that neither side was sincere. The Covenanters did not disband their army and Charles insisted on the inclusion of bishops in the forthcoming General Assembly. In August 1639, despite the fact that the king had returned to London, a new General Assembly met in Edinburgh, re-enacted the acts of the Glasgow Assembly and declared bishops not merely to be contrary to the laws of the church, but contrary to the law of God (a direct challenge to the king who appointed them). The parliament that met in Edinburgh later in the month confirmed the General Assembly's acts and, when the king ordered its prorogation, argued that it could not be prorogued without its own consent. It did, however, cease meeting and appointed representatives to carry on business until it should next meet.

The king was taken up with matters in England while the Covenanters mustered their forces and, in August 1640, the Scots army crossed the River Tweed and headed towards Newcastle. The English army was commanded by the inexperienced earl of Northumberland, whose mutinous troops violently clashed with the local civilians. The English forces were routed at Newburn, while citizens of nearby Newcastle (who had already displayed their opposition to the king's policies) welcomed the Scots army. Even the citizens of London greeted the Scots' victory with joy. The king's forces in Scotland proved unable to defend Edinburgh, and in October 1640 negotiations between king and Covenanters opened in Ripon, Yorkshire. The settlement they agreed required the king to pay the Scots army £850 a day as long as it remained on English soil, a sum which Charles could not raise without raising new taxes through parliament.

EXERCISE

Think now about these events in the light of our themes: state formation and beliefs and ideologies. I suggested in Unit 9 that Scotland could not claim to be a fully fledged state, but the actions of the Scots suggest that they regarded themselves as sovereign over such matters as the control of the church. Were ideas about the state driving religious changes or was religion the motive for demands about secular power?

Spend just a few minutes on this exercise.

SPECIMEN ANSWER

It is very hard to say which came first. Charles felt entitled to govern the Scottish church without either the intervention of the ecclesiastical power (the General Assembly) or the secular power (the Scottish parliament). For many Scots, however, especially the most ardent supporters of the Covenant, the idea of the church being governed by a secular power was abhorrent (hence the declaration that bishops, appointed by the king, were against the law of God). For them, the proper government of the church was through the Presbyterian parish assemblies representing the sum of believers. But this was not a democratic ideology, it was a theocratic one.

DISCUSSION

Apart from the difficulty of disentangling religious and secular motivations, we might want to ask whether the First and Second Bishops' Wars could be construed as wars of self-determination. They were certainly inspired by a violent reaction against the imposition of English religious innovations. The Scots then limited the king's power by statute, placing him *under* the law. So the National Covenant is sometimes regarded as a nationalist declaration, for the movement it inspired was not solely religious.

The Short Parliament and the early months of the Long Parliament

We left Charles in England governing without parliament, with an income raised by a variety of contrivances and Archbishop Laud embarking on church reforms that roused popular opposition and encouraged sympathy for the Scots. But what impact did the Scots rebellion have on the fragile balance of Charles's relations with his English subjects? (We are retracing our steps to before the First Bishops' War, so look at the chronology on the A200 website to see how these events fit together.)

The Scots mobilisation in the spring of 1639 required the king immediately to raise an army; with no money to pay it he was forced to conclude the pacification of Berwick. In the autumn of 1639, his close ally Thomas Wentworth returned to London from Dublin and, in anticipation of further trouble in Scotland, advised him to call the English parliament, which, Wentworth believed, could be managed to fund an effective campaign against the Scots.

MPs who met in April 1640 lost no time in reviewing the wrongs. As the earl of Clarendon (an MP in this parliament) wrote many years later:

> Mr Pym, a man of good reputation ... brake the ice; and, in a set discourse of above two hours, after mention of the King with the most profound reverence and commendation of his wisdom and justice, he observed that by the long intermission of Parliaments many unwarrantable things had been practised, notwithstanding the great virtue of his majesty: and then enumerated all the projects which had been set on foot, all the illegal proclamations which had been published and the proceedings which had been upon those proclamations, the judgment upon ship-money, and many grievances which related to the ecclesiastical jurisdiction; summing up shortly

and sharply all that most reflected upon the prudence and justice of
the government; concluding, that he had only laid that scheme before
them that they might see how much work they had to do to satisfy
their country.

(Clarendon, 1888, vol. 1, pp. 174–5)

> **John Pym** (1584–1643) first sat as an MP in 1614 and emerged in the 1620s as
> an opponent of the king. He was unofficial leader of the House of Commons in
> the Short Parliament and remained a leading figure in the early years of the
> Long Parliament. He was one of the five MPs the king attempted to arrest in
> January 1642. After the outbreak of war he advocated outright military victory
> for parliament and fostering the Scots alliance.

Charles required £100,000 a month to fund the army, but he received little
sympathy from parliament. The House of Commons wanted consideration of
its grievances and announced that 'Till the liberties of the House and kingdom
were cleared, they knew not whether they had anything to give or no' (quoted
in Woolrych, 2002, p. 136). While Wentworth (now earl of Strafford)
attempted to persuade the House of Lords to support the king, Lord Saye and
Sele argued strongly for the right of the House of Commons to initiate votes of
taxation. Strafford's strategy divided the Lords and sowed dissention between
the two houses.

The Commons also questioned the king's right to commission Convocation
(the governing body of the Church of England) to prepare new ecclesiastical
canons embodying the changes intended 'to expel irreverence and profaneness'
and to return the church 'unto the former splendour of uniformity, devotion
and holy order, the lustre whereof for some years bypast hath been much
obscured' (Bray, 1998, p. 556). In short, the canons were to do away with the
practices beloved of Puritans who wanted more preaching and less ceremony
and to make law the reforms that Archbishop Laud had started. Debates in
parliament established the strength of the opposition to the proposed reforms
and there were sympathetic exchanges between some MPs and the rebellious
Scots. A further royal demand for supply was followed by parliamentary
procrastination, so the king dissolved parliament after three weeks, without a
single measure being agreed.

Strafford advised Charles that a forced loan raised from the City of London
and improved collection of ship money would support a short, sharp war to
crush the Scots. The earl then uttered the fateful words 'You have an army in
Ireland you may employ here to reduce this kingdom', words which were
almost certainly intended to mean reducing Scotland but which were
understood by the king's opponents, to whom they were leaked, to mean his
English subjects.

As we have seen, war with the Scots recommenced in the summer of 1640
and it soon became obvious that there was insufficient money to pay an army.

A peace settlement was concluded with the Scots at Ripon in October 1640, and a new parliament met in London in November. The elections caused considerable excitement. In many constituencies several candidates contested each seat (earlier in the century it was quite usual for there to be only one candidate). The franchise consisted of men of property, a minority of the adult population (see Unit 9, Table 9.1, for the details). Throughout England and Wales, public petitions presented to parliamentary candidates alluded to the threat to true religion, the long intervals between parliaments, and infractions of the rule of law during the personal rule.

The new parliament awakened high hopes in England and Wales, while the Scots hoped to see the reforms they had pushed through the Edinburgh parliament replicated in Westminster. Thomas Knyvett, a Norfolk gentleman, wrote home from London that 'reformation goes on again as hot as toast' (quoted in Coward, 1994 [1980], p. 189). Members were intent upon dismantling the hated changes of the last eleven years and they turned first against the man regarded as the chief architect, the earl of Strafford, adopting the expedient formula that it was not the king but the 'evil counsels' of his ministers that were responsible for the assaults on ancient liberties. John Pym, who had opened the Short Parliament with a lengthy and measured account of grievances, four days into the new parliament, exclaimed '[There is] a design to alter the kingdom both in religion and government. This is the highest of treason' (Kenyon, 1986 [1965], p. 189).

In the packed months that followed, the judges who had ruled in favour of ship money were impeached, Archbishop Laud was imprisoned, and Strafford's trial began, the principal charges against him being that he had sowed discord between king and people, had erected 'arbitrary and tyrannical government' in the north of England and in Ireland, and provoked the Second Bishops' War (Kenyon, 1986 [1965], p. 178). The prosecution found it impossible to convince an overall majority of Commons or Lords that Strafford was guilty of treason. The Commons were determined and passed an Act of Attainder asserting Strafford's guilt and sentencing him to death. Under the threat of violence, the king signed the Act, agreeing at the same time that parliament could not be dissolved without its own consent. He went on to sign: an Act abolishing the hated prerogative courts of High Commission and Star Chamber (which had been used to effect against his opponents); an Act against ship money; and a Triennial Act requiring a meeting of parliament for at least fifty days in every three-year period. Parliament discussed whether they should insist that royal counsellors be men in whom parliament had confidence (they stopped short of the Scots position under which the Scottish parliament could control the appointment of ministers).

At the same time, parliament condemned the newly issued English ecclesiastical canons and, in December 1640, a petition from London was presented to the House of Commons declaring that:

> whereas the government of archbishops and lord bishops, deans and archdeacons, etc., with their courts and ministrations in them, have

proved prejudicial and very dangerous both to the Church and Commonwealth ... And whereas the said government is found by woeful experience to be a main cause and occasion of many foul evils ...

We therefore most humbly pray and beseech this honourable assembly ... that the said government, with all its dependencies, roots and branches, may be abolished.

(Kenyon, 1986 [1965], p. 154)

Several counties produced similar petitions and, in May 1641, a Bill to remove bishops 'root and branch' was moved in parliament. But by this time, it had become clear that MPs were deeply divided about how to settle the church, and counter-petitions in favour of bishops began to arrive. Strafford's trial had also split parliament and a party supporting the king had started to emerge. It was at this moment that news reached London of the outbreak of rebellion in Ireland.

EXERCISE

Reflecting on what you have read in the last section, list the characteristics of the development in parliament of opposition to the king?

Spend just a few minutes on this exercise.

SPECIMEN ANSWER

At the first meeting of the Short Parliament, MPs were unified by their demand for the redress of grievances, notably stopping the king from raising taxation without parliament's consent and reforming the church. But Strafford's policy of trying to divide parliament was successful, and by the time he was put on trial there was a considerable body of support for the king from MPs and lords who feared that matters were going too far. By the time the new parliament met, a party in support of the king, bishops and Strafford had started to emerge.

Ireland and 1641

Despite its proximity to England and movement between the two kingdoms, Ireland was an object of almost anthropological curiosity. English rulers had, since Henry VIII declared himself king of Ireland in 1541, considered the place to be the haunt of barbarians. Rebellions by Gaelic lords in the late sixteenth century had established in many English minds that the Catholic Irish were not to be trusted. The government expropriated rebels' land and instituted schemes to grant it to Protestant English and Scots settlers (planters), extending the region of Protestant settlement from the area surrounding Dublin to King's and Queen's counties (Counties Laois and Offaly), parts of the province of Munster, and substantial tracts of Ulster.

Much of the writing about the country either expatiated on the quaintness of the Irish (in the hopes of encouraging English families to settle there) or on a lack of civility (providing authors with opportunities to describe Irish lasciviousness and the dirt in which they lived for the amusement of an English audience and justifying the seizure of land from rebel leaders).

A characteristic description is that of Barnaby Rich, an English soldier who spent much of his later life in Ireland where he wrote several books, some complimentary and some not.

Read Anthology Document 3.8, 'The nature of the Irish, 1610'. What impression does Rich convey of the Irish?

Spend about 15 minutes on this exercise.

Rich starts by saying how similar the English, Scots and Irish were, and how superior to other races. But he quickly remarks on the uncivilised dress of the Irish from the remote parts and on undesirable qualities of character, which he attributes to their Catholicism or, rather, their adherence to the pope in preference to the government of the king of England.

As we saw in Unit 9, Ireland was a complex, multicultural society of Gaelic Irish, Old English, New English and Scots. In 1628, Charles I recognised the loyal protestations of the Old English by assuring them, in a document known as the Graces, of titles to land they had occupied undisputed for more than sixty years and by no longer requiring of heirs that they take the Oath of Supremacy, which was unacceptable to Catholics because it declared the monarch to be head of the Church of England/Ireland. It was agreed that, in return, the Irish parliament (which was traditionally dominated by the Old English) would grant the king revenue.

Charles I had little knowledge of Ireland. In 1633, he sent Thomas Wentworth to Dublin as lord deputy, knowing that Wentworth would wish to carry out the 'policy of thorough' to improve the administrative efficiency of the government and, more important, to increase tax revenues. Wentworth wanted also to reform the church and improve the position of Church of Ireland bishops, but his reference in a letter to his friend Archbishop Laud to 'reducing this kingdom to a conformity in religion with the church in England' reveals that this was not to be achieved by negotiation (Knowler, 1740, vol. 1, p. 187).

In 1634, Wentworth called a parliament in Dublin. The Old English members wanted to grant him subsidies in return for the ratification of the Graces; the New English settlers, however, believed that a better way of raising money would be stricter enforcement of fines levied from Catholics for not attending Protestant Church of Ireland services. Wentworth managed to alienate both communities by meddling with payments for office-holding in the Dublin government (antagonising the New English), and attempting to reclaim Church of Ireland land that had been redistributed among the laity. Wentworth's particular crime, in the eyes of the inhabitants of Ireland, though, was to regard the country as a source of men and money to help the king out of his troubles in his other kingdoms.

In October 1641, unanticipated by the governments in either Dublin or London, the Catholic Irish in Ulster erupted in rebellion (see Figure 10.8). 'The uprising in Ulster was not the response to some specific English act or policy, but rather an outburst against immemorial grievances ... .

[The conspirators'] motives were as vague as their plans' (Bottigheimer, 1971, pp. 30–1). Parliament in London prepared to ask the City of London for a loan of £50,000 to fund an army to be sent to Ireland.

Had the rising been confined to Ulster, matters would have been relatively straightforward, but in December 1641 the Old English (a group traditionally loyal to the crown, though largely Catholic) joined the rebels. The historian Nicholas Canny characterises the change as 'nothing short of a revolution', but one which was out of the control of the original leaders, who were unable to restrain the outburst of popular fury by native Irish against the Protestant settler communities of Ulster, Munster and Leinster (Canny, 1987, p. 208). The violence of the rising was branded on everyone's consciousnesses: estimates of the number of Protestants killed range from 4,000 (by historians) to 200,000 (by propagandists). Undoubtedly many more people died from famine and pestilence, and from the theft and destruction of livestock and crops.

This episode looms large in the consciousness of Ulster Protestants to this day and it is one whose history is difficult to write dispassionately, since virtually all the surviving testimony comes from Protestants' sworn depositions about the injury and loss they had suffered, often taken some years after the event.

EXERCISE

Read Anthology Document 3.9, 'Protestant depositions in Ireland, 1641', extracts (a) and (b).

1   What can we tell about the deponents themselves?

2   Are these accounts likely to be accurate in all particulars?

Spend about 20 minutes on this exercise.

SPECIMEN ANSWER

1   We know that these deponents were women and were all unable to write their names (from which we may deduce that the accounts were written down by clerks). One deponent was the widow of an inn-keeper and evidently quite prosperous.

2   Both accounts contain a good deal of hearsay evidence and the similarities in the accounts, given that the women had not written them down themselves, might give rise to the suspicion that the clerks who recorded the depositions used stock phrases. But both accounts are extremely specific, naming Catholic rebels, people who were neighbours and known to the deponents, and providing details about places. Nevertheless, bearing in mind Rich's account of the Irish, it is difficult not to suspect some stereotyping of what the rebellious Irish were expected to do.

DISCUSSION

Despite their one-sided view of the events of 1641, these depositions are an extremely important historical source for the history of the rising because there is so little other material. They identify by name many of the rebels, they provide some eye-witness accounts, and tell us about the mentality of the Protestant settlers, many of them people of humble circumstances. However, they also contain a great deal of hearsay evidence, and testimony within them was repeated – and often embellished – in propaganda pamphlets produced for a fearful English audience (Gibney, 2011, pp. 71–2) (see Figure 10.8).

Figure 10.8 Illustrations from *The Teares of Ireland wherein is lively presented as in a map, a list of the unheard off cruelties and perfidious treacheries of bloud-thirsty Jesuits and the Popish faction*, London, A. N. for John Rothwell, 1642, p. 23. Photo: The British Library. This is one of the more luridly illustrated of the many accounts of the Catholic assaults on Protestants in the early months of the rising

The spread of the rebellion beyond Ulster increased the urgency of defeating the insurgents, and to do this the king had to have an army. In November 1641, parliament at Westminster resolved to send 12,000 men from England and to ask the Scots to send 10,000 more. Some troops arrived in Ireland in January 1642, and 2,500 Scots finally arrived in Ireland in April. It was not until February that parliament in London passed, and the king signed, an Act for Reducing Ireland under which individuals would advance money to suppress the rebellion and in exchange be guaranteed lands in Ireland from those yet to be confiscated from the undefeated rebels. Slowly, an army was gathered in England under the command of Philip Lord Wharton, but in July 1642 his officers were ordered by parliament to remain in England to serve against the king. It was not until 1649 that a serious attempt was made from England to defeat the Irish rebels.

CONCLUSION

The causes of the Civil Wars have been a subject for debate virtually since they began. Rushworth and Nalson, extracts from whose histories you read in Unit 9, were writing about them in the seventeenth century. You will remember that both wrote their accounts, as they saw it, to set the record straight. And such differences continue to the present day.

EXERCISE

Re-read Austin Woolrych, 'Shifting perspectives on the Great Rebellion' (which you accessed via the A200 website in Unit 9), and the set book, Wallace, pp. 138–9.

1   What different approaches to the causes of the Civil Wars does Woolrych describe? (Try to think of broader categories rather than the individual historians.)

2   What approach does Wallace adopt?

Spend about 20 minutes on this exercise.

SPECIMEN ANSWER

1   Woolrych describes three main approaches.

(a) Those derived from the interest of historians in whether different social classes were on the decline or the ascendant. For some historians, the primary interest has been in the economic dominance of one class or another. This is an approach often associated with Marxist interpretations of history. For others, it has been to do with the political influence to which different classes had access.

(b) The detailed, empirical studies of the personnel of English politics, whether in parliament, the royal administration or the City of London, on the one hand, or in local government in the counties, on the other.

(c) The studies of events in Scotland and Ireland that draw attention to the interconnectedness of developments in the three kingdoms.

2   Inevitably, Wallace emphasises the religious causes (though he mentions the constitutional discontents of the 1630s). He mentions differences between Protestants in England and Scotland, and the differences between Protestants and Catholics in Ireland.

The debate that has taken place over the causes of the Civil Wars has been not so much between these different groups of historians as within them. You can see that the Marxist interpretation has influenced many historians who were not or are not themselves Marxist. The studies of the personnel of English politics have led to strongly worded debates about the role of the House of Lords and its relationship with the House of Commons in the 1640s. County studies have drawn attention to the strength of the neutralist movements (those who said 'a plague on both your houses') and to the variety of local conditions and allegiances that might affect individuals' choices. You saw, in Unit 9, something of the substance of 'the new British history', and earlier in this unit you have seen the way in which the Bishops' Wars and the Ulster Rising affected developments in England.

The Civil Wars began as a result of a series of complicated events driven by irreconcilable attitudes to religion and royal power. Opposition concentrated around the king's ideology of rule and the organisation and practices of the church. There seems to have been little disagreement about the existence of a monarchical state; even in 1642, no one expected much more than modest reforms. The idea of a revolution and the overthrow of the monarchy was far from their minds.

REFERENCES

Bottigheimer, K.S. (1971) *English Money and Irish Land*, Oxford, Oxford University Press.

Braddick, M. (1996) *The Nerves of State: Taxation and the Financing of the English State, 1558–1714*, Manchester, Manchester University Press.

Bray, G. (ed.) (1998) *The Anglican Canons 1529–1947*, Church of England Record Society, vol. 6, Woodbridge, Boydell Press.

Canny, N. (1987) *From Reformation to Restoration: Ireland, 1534–1660*, Dublin, Helicon Press.

Clarendon, Edward Hyde, earl of (1888) *The History of the Rebellion and Civil Wars in England* (ed. W. Dunn Macray), 6 vols, Oxford, Clarendon Press.

Coward, B. (1994 [1980]) *The Stuart Age*, 2nd edn, Harlow, Longman.

Donaldson, G. (1978 [1965]) *Scotland: James V–James VII*, Edinburgh History of Scotland, vol.3, Edinburgh, Oliver and Boyd.

Fincham, K. and Tyacke, N. (2007) *Altars Restored: The Changing Face of English Worship, 1547–c.1700*, Oxford, Oxford University Press.

Foster, W.R. (1975) *The Church before the Covenants: The Church of Scotland 1596–1638*, Edinburgh, Scottish Academic Press.

Fyfe, J.G. (ed.) (1928) *Scottish Diaries and Memoirs 1550–1746*, Stirling, Eneas Mackay.

Gibney, J. (2011) 'Protestant interests? The 1641 rebellion and state formation in early modern Ireland', *Historical Research*, vol. 84, no. 223, pp. 67–86.

Haigh, C. (2007) *The Plain Man's Pathways to Heaven: Kinds of Christianity in Post-Reformation England, 1570–1640*, Oxford, Oxford University Press.

Hobsbawm, E. (1974 [1954]) 'The crisis of the seventeenth century' in Aston, T. (ed.) *Crisis in Europe 1560–1660: Essays from Past and Present*, London, Routledge and Kegan Paul, pp. 1–58.

Kenyon, J.P. (1986 [1965]) *The Stuart Constitution 1603–1688: Documents and Commentary*, 2nd edn, Cambridge, Cambridge University Press.

Knowler, W. (ed.) (1740) *The Earl of Strafford's Letters and Dispatches*, 2 vols, Dublin.

Laud, W. (1847–60) *The Works of the Most Reverend Father in God*, 9 vols, Oxford, J.H. Parker.

Lee, M. (1984) 'Scotland and the "general crisis" of the seventeenth century', *Scottish Historical Review*, vol. 63, pp. 136–54.

Morrill, J. (1993 [1984]) 'The religious context of the English civil war' in Morrill, J., *The Nature of the English Revolution*, London, Longman, pp. 45–68.

Ó hAnnracháin, T. (2002) *Catholic Reformation in Ireland: The Mission of Riniccini 1645–1649*, Oxford, Oxford University Press.

Parker, G. and Smith, L. (1978) 'Introduction' in Parker, G. and Smith, L. (eds) *The General Crisis of the Seventeenth Century*, London, Routledge and Kegan Paul, pp. 1–25.

Scott, J. (2000) *England's Troubles: Seventeenth-Century English Political Instability in European Context*, Cambridge, Cambridge University Press.

Sharpe, K. (1992) *The Personal Rule of Charles I*, New Haven and London, Yale University Press.

Stone, L. (1972) *Causes of the English Revolution*, London, Routledge and Kegan Paul.

Tawney, R.H. (1928) *English Constitutional Conflicts of the Seventeenth Century 1603–89*, Cambridge, Cambridge University Press.

Trevor-Roper, H. (1974 [1959]) 'The general crisis of the seventeenth century' in Aston, T. (ed.) *Crisis in Europe 1560–1660: Essays from Past and Present*, London, Routledge and Kegan Paul, pp. 59–95.

Woolrych, A. (2002) *Britain in Revolution 1625–60*, Oxford, Oxford University Press.

Anne Laurence and Rachel C. Gibbons

INTRODUCTION

By far the most significant event of the war in England and its aftermath was the execution of the king on 30 January 1649. Despite the fact that many people were convinced that the only hope of peace was to be rid of a weak and duplicitous ruler, there was a terrible shock as the executioner's axe fell. At that moment, in the words of a witness to the scene, there went up 'such a groan as I never heard before, and desire that I may never hear again' (Wedgwood, 1971 [1964], p. 219). The archbishop of Armagh, James Ussher, saw the preliminaries of the execution from the roof of Lady Peterborough's house in St Martin's Lane, but fainted when 'the villains in vizards began to put up his hair' (*Dictionary of National Biography on CD-ROM*, 1988, 'Ussher').

But did Charles's execution have the same impact in his other two kingdoms? His heir, Prince Charles, was declared king in Scotland (parliament in England had hastily declared it illegal to proclaim anyone king after Charles I's execution) and was crowned a few months before the Scots were defeated decisively by the English at the battle of Worcester in 1651. In 1649, a substantial part of Ireland was under the control of the Catholic Confederation of Kilkenny, which had concluded a truce with the earl of Ormond and the royal forces he commanded there. Perhaps the most emblematic event of the period in Ireland was the capture of Drogheda by parliament's forces in 1649 and the massacre there – the prelude to the victory of parliament over both the Catholic rebels and the royalist forces in Ireland.

A unit of this length cannot hope to cover all the ins and outs of the wars and their aftermath, so it concentrates on those aspects of the wars that relate most closely to the themes of the module. We shall also see rather more of events in England than in Scotland and Ireland. While the general subject of the unit is how the Wars of the Three Kingdoms led to the execution of the king, it focuses on:

- how the divisions between the combatants were dictated by their beliefs and ideologies
- how warfare affected producers and consumers
- whether the nature of the state altered in the 1650s.

As well as thinking about the Wars of the Three Kingdoms, you will work on a selection of documents and use the online *Oxford Dictionary of National Biography.*

BELIEFS AND IDEOLOGIES IN THE WARS 1642–49

The historian Conrad Russell noted that, whatever the longer term causes of conflict might have been, it was the failure of the political process that forced the taking up of arms in England in 1642, for many of the subjects about which the two sides disagreed had divided them for a long time (Russell, 1990, p. 19). We might also argue that it was the failure of the political process in Scotland and Ireland that led to Scots and Irish taking up arms against the English in 1638 and 1641, respectively. Certainly the difficulties of balancing the claims of three kingdoms, each with a distinctive religious character, with his own convictions about the nature of kingship and the church, placed demands on Charles that he was ill placed to meet. Having got to the point of war, however, some kind of conviction kept men fighting, and in this section we shall look at the beliefs and ideologies that divided the parties.

Taking sides: England 1642–43

The last unit ended in July 1642 with the army commanded by Lord Wharton, raised to put down the Irish rebellion, being ordered to remain in England by parliament in order to confront forces raised by Charles I. How had matters degenerated over just a few months to the brink of civil war between king and parliament? Despite the victory of John Pym MP and his parliamentary allies in forcing the attainder and execution of Strafford in May 1641 and several legislative concessions from the king (see Unit 10, p. 54), many in parliament were still suspicious of Charles's policies towards the church, and the private religious beliefs of him, his French wife and children. The uprising in Ireland had heightened fears of a popish conspiracy and, in December 1641, parliament presented the king with their Grand Remonstrance (passed by eleven votes) setting out further demands over matters of religion. Anthology Document 3.10, 'Extracts from the Grand Remonstrance, 1641' provides an extract.

The Grand Remonstrance listed those who were considered responsible for 'subverting the fundamental laws and principles of government': Jesuits and papists, bishops and the corrupt part of the clergy, courtiers who had 'engaged themselves to foreign princes'. It called for a synod of divines from England and other Protestant countries to advise on settling the church, for the effective execution of the laws against papists and for the king to appoint only such ministers as parliament might have confidence in 'without which we cannot give his majesty such supplies for support of its own estate, nor such assistance to the Protestant party beyond the sea, as is desired' (Gardiner, 1906 [1889], pp. 202–32). Rioting in London and the gathering of soldiers to join Wharton's force for Ireland increased tension and Charles, in one of his most unwise moves, attempted in January 1642 to seize and impeach five MPs and one peer on the grounds that they (repeating the words of the Grand Remonstrance) had attempted to subvert the laws of the kingdom. Forewarned, the men had absented themselves from parliament. Meanwhile, parliament was working on a bill to allow it (rather than the king) to nominate the lords lieutenant (the royal official in each county responsible for levying the militia). Charles refused to sign the bill and retreated to York. Parliament passed the bill as an ordinance (a law without royal assent) and nominated new lords lieutenant. Further negotiations took place culminating in the Nineteen Propositions in which parliament increased its demands beyond those of the Grand Remonstrance, calling on the king to place his children's upbringing and marriages in the hands of parliament. Shortly after, the king issued his own commissions of array to gentlemen in the shires, implicitly setting aside the Militia Ordinance and ordering the mustering of forces in each English and Welsh county to create his own army. We can get a sense of the relative strength of feeling for each side by looking at where the measures were implemented.

EXERCISE

Look at the *Visual Sources Book*, Plates 11.1 and 11.2.

1   What do you notice about the strength of support for parliament's Militia Ordinance?

2   What do you notice about the strength of support for the king's Commissions of Array?

Spend about 15 minutes on this exercise.

SPECIMEN ANSWER

1   The Militia Ordinance was implemented in fourteen counties between May and July and a further nine between August and October, out of a possible forty counties in England. The counties were predominantly in the east and south of England. It was not implemented in any of the twelve Welsh counties.

2   Commissions of Array were executed in ten English counties, predominantly in the north and west of the country, and one Welsh county. Commissions failed in a further twelve counties, predominantly in the Midlands.

DISCUSSION

From this one would deduce that there was stronger support for parliament than for the king. However, the four most northerly counties followed neither set of instructions, nor did Dorset, Derbyshire, Huntingdonshire or most of Wales. In five counties, both the Militia Ordinance and the Commissions of Array were fully executed, and in a further six counties attempts were made to execute both. We should not assume that in those counties where neither measure was implemented the population was simply indifferent; the Staffordshire gentry were determined to remain neutral. The maps show that the population of England and Wales was not clearly divided between king and parliament and they hint at, but do not allow us accurately to predict, the geography of allegiance that was to emerge by the mid-1640s.

For those who were actively involved as MPs, or who had to respond either to parliament's Militia Ordinance or to the king's Commissions of Array, or who had particularly strong religious convictions, the war started in August 1642. Two-thirds of peers joined the king, but a majority of the House of Commons supported parliament. Both peers and MPs raised troops for the army. For the vast majority of other people, the war started a good deal later, as the leading historian of localism in the Civil Wars has written, 'Less than one third of the supporters of each side actually took up a military or civilian position in the years 1643–5 ... The bulk of the gentry were reluctantly involved in the conflict' (Morrill, 1974, pp. 73, 74). And, of the moderates, he said, 'the hallmark of the moderate was that he wanted to obey *both* sides, not *neither*, and when one side issued a direct and personal order he acquiesced. Those not directly charged by either side could and did continue to sit on the fence' (Morrill, 1976, p. 42). Many participants were as much preoccupied with local divisions as with events taking place in London or the king's headquarters at Oxford.

Nonetheless, much of England did mobilise, many thousands of people did go to war and many died as a result. Why was it that they felt so passionately that they were prepared to risk their lives? Actually taking up arms not just against your ruler, but also against your fellow citizens, is a far cry from objecting to unjust exactions. These were not just tax riots or popular demonstrations; this was a substantial part of the political nation, the people in whose hands the government of the country rested, mobilising an army against similar people.

What persuaded people to join one side or the other? Just as the English population at the time of the Wars of the Roses (Block 1, pp. 74–92) found it difficult to take sides, so did the English population in 1642. The allegiances of men such as John Pym and John Hampden were not in doubt, nor were those closely connected with the royal court. The ironworkers of Birmingham, 'then a small town noted for its Puritanism and its ironwork', made up their minds quickly and supplied the earl of Essex, commander-in-chief of parliament's forces, with 15,000 sword blades and imprisoned the messengers who brought royal orders to make weapons for the king (Gardiner, 1893, vol. 1, p. 107). But for the vast majority of people, the decision was not so straightforward. Barbara Donegan argues that 'probably the majority of the population ... initially put peace and quiet above principle and hoped to evade choice between sides' (Donegan, 2007, p. 66). Conrad Russell makes the important point that confessional allegiance was not identical with political allegiance, that is to say that not everyone who disapproved of the king's religious policies necessarily felt that it was legitimate to take up arms against the divinely ordained monarch, while not everyone who objected to the king's bending of the constitution revolted against his religious policies (Russell, 1990, p. 20). Many people took a long time to decide for one side or the other and it has become evident, through the excellent county histories that have been published for many English (though few Welsh or Scottish) counties, that local politics could influence allegiances.

EXERCISE

Now read Andy Wood, 'Beyond post-revisionism? The Civil War allegiances of the miners of the Derbyshire "Peak country"', in the Block 3 secondary sources on the A200 website. As with other online resources, you can either read the article onscreen or print it out. Concentrate on pp. 28–36.

How does Wood characterise the miners' allegiance?

Spend around 30 minutes on this exercise.

Wood suggests that the miners were politicised by challenges from landowners to their rights to work independently, but that religion (in particular Puritanism) had little impact on them (here Wood contrasts his view with those of other historians). On p. 32, Wood draws attention to the incentives offered by the king to miners and concludes (p. 35) that they were actually deeply divided between king and parliament.

If we consider Wood's findings alongside the maps at which you have just looked (*Visual Sources Book*, Plates 11.1 and 11.2), it is clear that people's choices and allegiances could be complex. However, it is apparent that many people saw the king's religious innovations as connected with his infringement of their ancient rights. And the religious aspect of the armies began to be evident from the early months of the war.

Having raised their armies, the forces of king and parliament took to the field. Their first major engagement, on 23 October 1642, was at Edgehill, Warwickshire, a county that was to be much fought over in the coming years. The result was inconclusive, but in one respect it set the tone for the rest of the war. The king's forces were commanded by his nephew Prince Rupert. They chased parliament's cavalry off the field, but instead of turning on the now unprotected infantry, set about plundering the district. Parliament's army (under the command of Robert Devereux, 3rd earl of Essex (1591–1646)) was addressed before the battle by chaplains who rode among the soldiers 'through the thickest dangers, and in much personal hazard, most faithfully and courageously exhorting and encouraging the soldiers to fight valiantly, and not to fly' (Vicars, 1644, p. 200).

Prince Rupert (1619–1682), third son of the elector Palatine and nephew of Charles I, received his military training in Germany in the 1630s. He arrived in England in July 1642, was made general of the king's horse and, in 1644, commander-in-chief of the king's army. Court-martialled after the loss of Bristol, he was restored to favour but left England after the fall of Oxford and joined the French service. In 1649, he commanded a naval expedition to Ireland and privateering expeditions across the Atlantic and elsewhere. He joined Charles II in exile and returned to England in 1660, when he served Charles in various capacities.

It suited the parliamentary cause to present such a clear dichotomy between the two sides – the God-fearing courageous Roundheads facing down the 'swearing, roaring, whoring Cavalier', as an anonymous pamphlet of 1642 put it (Memegalos, 2007, p. 125 and n. 56). However, in the same way that decisions on whether to put king before parliament – or even whether to choose at all – could be complex, so too were the people behind those choices.

EXERCISE

Turn to *Visual Sources Book*, Plates 10.1(c) and (d), which are two portraits by the celebrated Flemish painter Sir Anthony Van Dyck (1599–1642). Examine the clothing, pose and general appearance of the subjects.

If you knew nothing about the men portrayed, who would you say was the 'Cavalier' and who the 'Roundhead', given popular perceptions? And why?

Spend about 5 minutes on this exercise.

SPECIMEN ANSWER

The attitudes, fine clothing and props in both paintings suggest men of culture and authority. The man in Plate 10.1(c) is flamboyantly posed and dressed, in luxurious scarlet embroidered with gold. His lace collar, goatee and styled moustache mimic those of Charles I himself (Plate 10.1(a)), so we can conclude he is a man of fashion, possibly a courtier. The seascape background and armour suggest a man of war/action too. Is he a Cavalier?

Conversely, the subject of 10.1(d) is depicted with his secretary, implying a man of serious business, perhaps a lawyer, MP or important government official. He is dressed soberly, in black with a plain linen collar, relatively short hair and neat beard; and, hence, one might presume he was of Puritan sympathies – and, therefore, at face value, perhaps *looks* like a Roundhead.

DISCUSSION

The caption under Plate 10.1(d) names the sitter as Thomas Wentworth, earl of Strafford – and, hence, from your work in Unit 10, you will know that he was not a parliamentarian, but one of the most loyal supporters of the king. Strafford was a soldier, lord lieutenant of Ireland, and was the figure on whom the Long Parliament focused its criticisms of royal policies in 1640, leading to his attainder and execution the following year.

Plate 10.1(c) depicts Robert Rich, earl of Warwick – and confirms that there was no stereotypical royalist or parliamentarian, and that appearances may be deceptive. Warwick was a powerful nobleman but grew increasingly hostile to Charles I's financial policies and Laudian church reforms during the 1630s. He pushed for Strafford's attainder in the House of Lords and, once war broke out, was a leading parliamentarian commander on land and sea.

The king's forces were not universally rapacious and irreligious, any more than parliament's forces were universally sober and godly. Barbara Donegan describes the royalists as a 'rainbow coalition ... that included men and women of strikingly diverse personalities' (2007, p. 66), and people from all classes were drawn to the parliamentarian cause. A Cambridgeshire gentleman, raising a force for parliament's East Anglian army in 1643, described what he was looking for:

> a few honest men are better than numbers ... If you choose godly honest men to be captains of horse, honest men will follow them ... I had rather have a plain russet-coated captain that knows what he fights for, and loves what he knows, than that which you call a gentleman and is nothing else.
>
> (quoted in Abbott, 1937, vol. 1, p. 256)

At the time that he wrote this, Oliver Cromwell was commander of a small force within the army of the Eastern Association, raised from the combined East Anglian counties and commanded by the earl of Manchester – an army subsidiary to the main forces under the earl of Essex.

> **Oliver Cromwell** (1599–1658) was an East Anglian gentleman and MP. In 1642, he joined Essex's army as captain of horse but transferred to the army of the Eastern Association, rising to become second in command to the earl of Manchester. When the New Model Army was formed in 1645, he was appointed lieutenant-general to Fairfax, which he remained until 1649. He was appointed lord lieutenant of Ireland and commander-in-chief of the expeditionary force there in 1649, but was recalled by parliament to lead the expedition to Scotland in 1650. He dissolved the Rump Parliament in 1653. Barebone's Parliament surrendered their powers to him as commander-in-chief of the army and officers drew up a constitution appointing Cromwell protector. In 1657, he was offered and declined the crown, but he did agree to nominate a successor – his son Richard.

Propaganda, news and the press

In 1640, the censorship of the press that had been strictly enforced (by bishops and the Company of Stationers) lapsed. There was a sudden explosion of print materials, especially weekly or bi-weekly newsbooks that reported the progress of the war, and which increasingly represented the views of different factions within the two main sides.

EXERCISE

Read Anthology Document 3.11, 'Newsbook accounts of an engagement at Warrington, 8 April 1643', extract (a) '*Mercurius Aulicus* (Royalist newsbook)'. In the *Module Companion* we provide you with a set of questions to use in looking at primary sources. To remind you of these, the exercise here is based on them.

1   What kind of document is it?
     (a)   Who wrote it?
     (b)   Who was the intended audience/why was it written?
     (c)   When was it written?
     (d)   What type of document (public, private, official, published, etc.) is it?

2   What is its historical context? (You might want to look at the relevant chronology on the A200 website.)

3   Are there comments you can make on specific points in the text?

4   What is its significance for the study of our period?

Spend about 20 minutes on this exercise.

1   It is a newsbook (newspaper).

   (a)   The author was presumably editor or publisher of the newsbook.
   (b)   The intended audience, the readership of the newsbook, was anyone who could afford to buy it.
   (c)   On or after 9 April 1643.
   (d)   It is a public document, published and sold; it is one issue of a series.

2   It provides an account of a military engagement in Cheshire between royalist and parliamentarian forces at a fairly early stage of the Civil Wars.

3   It was intended to celebrate the earl of Derby's victory, gained by a rather underhand subterfuge, and the defeat of the parliamentary forces under Brereton.

4   Even though this is a very small extract, we can deduce from its highly partisan account of the engagement that this was probably a royalist newsbook. So an important general point to make is that this was a war in which printed propaganda featured significantly.

We cannot assume that the readership was royalist because, though this particular newsbook was published in Oxford (the king's headquarters), there was a lively market in newsbooks and *Mercurius Aulicus* could also be obtained in London.

It is unlikely that the authors of the newsbook accounts were correspondents on the battlefields sending back reports to their editors in Oxford or London. It is much more likely that the newsbooks used official reports of the war and letters from the generals carried by scouts to London and Oxford. You can see, in Anthology Document 3.11, extract (b) '*The Kingdomes Weekly Intelligencer* (Parliamentarian newsbook)' and extract (c) '*A Continuation of certaine Speciall and Remarkable Passages from both Houses of Parliament*', corresponding accounts of the same episode from the parliamentary press. In considering the passage's significance for the study of our period, we have not focused on the specific information about the engagement in Cheshire. Information about what happened where is normally a matter of public record, but what we are concerned with here is the way in which this document was used for propaganda.

We might want to note the different use of the word 'perfected'. (You can always check on the meaning of obscure words by looking them up in the *Oxford English Dictionary* online, through the Open University online library. It is particularly valuable for looking up ancient meanings.)

The outpouring of publications was not restricted to newsbooks. Pamphlets on religious and political subjects, and satirical and polemical ballads and tracts poured off the presses. Illustrations played an important part in the more popular works, though it is questionable how far they were intended for an illiterate population because the pictures often contained text (see Figure 11.1). Particular subjects for illustration were atrocities (see Figure 10.8) and portraits of victorious generals.

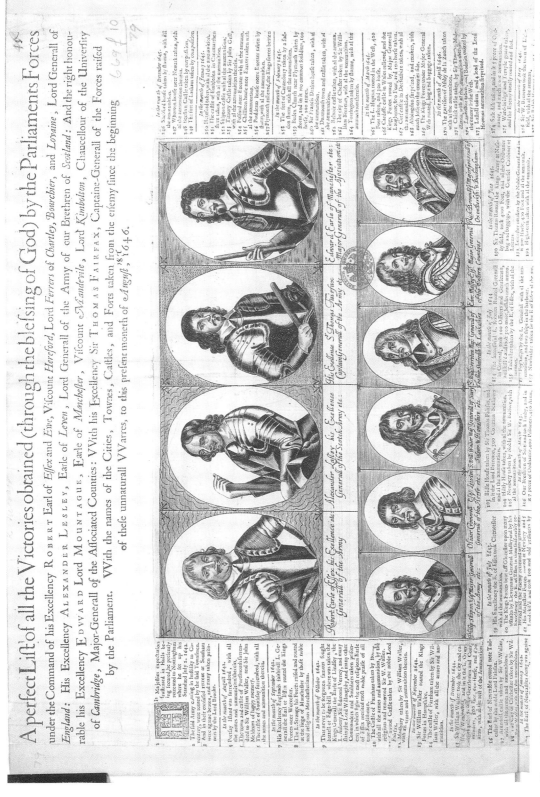

Figure 11.1 Josiah Ricraft, *A perfect List of all the Victories obtained (through the blessing of God) by the Parliaments Forces*, London, 1646. Photo: The British Library. London printers produced broadsheets listing victories and extolling the virtues of the parliamentarian generals

Divisions among the parliamentarians 1642–48

The press was used not only to put out propaganda on behalf of the main protagonists in the conflict in England, but also in connection with the growing divisions among the supporters of parliament. For the most part, the king's supporters had an overwhelming sense that to rebel against the king was not simply treason, it was an offence against God. A good many of his supporters had opposed the religious innovations in the 1630s, but felt unable to take up arms against a king who held his powers from God, and there was a steady trickle of defections from parliament to the king among peers and MPs, many of them during 1643, the year of parliament's greatest military failure.

From the outset of the war, the parliamentary cause was far more of a coalition of competing interests than was the king's. The motives of parliament's supporters were more complicated and various than the loyalty to kingly rule that animated most royalists. For some people, the king's crimes against his subjects were offences against their ancient liberties as 'freeborn Englishmen'. They associated the king with economic changes that had worked to their detriment, such as the reduction in the amount of common land, the imposition of oppressive taxes and a lack of regard for freedoms that were guaranteed by the Magna Carta. For others, he had offended against their idea of rightly reformed Protestant religion by pressing forward with Laudian innovations.

Parliament's military failures of 1643 prompted them to seek an alliance with the Scots, who themselves wanted to guarantee the religious changes for which they had fought the Bishops' Wars. The treaty with the Scots, the Solemn League and Covenant, was ratified by parliament in September 1643. Pressure to conclude it came from events in Ireland, where soldiers became available to join the royal army in England by a cessation of arms between the king's Irish forces and the Catholic rebels. There were two parts to the Scots' treaty: a military alliance under which the Scots provided a substantial army to serve and be paid for by parliament, and an agreement about the future of religion in England and Ireland.

EXERCISE	Now read Anthology Document 3.12, 'The religious provisions of the Solemn League and Covenant, September 1643' (see also Figure 11.2). What were the implications of the Solemn League and Covenant for the future of religion in England? Spend about 10 minutes on this exercise.
SPECIMEN ANSWER	The English agreed to defend the reforms of the Church of Scotland implemented after 1639 (no bishops, no Book of Common Prayer) and to preserve reformed religion in England and Ireland. The definition of reformed religion 'according to the Word of God and the example of the best reformed churches in Europe' might seem to have offered scope for flexibility, but there is also a requirement to bring the three churches 'to the nearest conjunction and uniformity'.
DISCUSSION	Given the opposition of many parliamentarians to the Laudian reforms in England, and the pledge in clause 2 to 'extirpate' (wipe out) the church hierarchy of bishops and other higher offices, there is little doubt that the uniformity being agreed to

here would be based on the Calvinist Church of Scotland, not the Church of England. It is revealing that the king's opponents shared something of his ambition that 'the Churches of God in the three kingdoms' should resemble as closely as possible one united church. Evidence would suggest, though, that their motivation came more from religious ideology – believing that a more Puritan church was 'of sound doctrine and the power of godliness' – than from seeking further to unify the three states, using the church as a mechanism of state formation, which Charles I certainly did.

The religious terms of the Scots alliance caused divisions among parliamentarians, which became more severe and more bitter as the years passed. The theocratic nature of the proposed ecclesiastical administration (giving overall responsibility to a general assembly of the church rather than parliament) was unpopular among many MPs and supporters of parliament. Attempts in 1643 and 1644 to ensure that all MPs, office holders and everyone with a military command had signed the Solemn League and Covenant met with some resistance.

We might view this division as a religious one, but it had political consequences, which we shall look at shortly. Another division that became apparent in 1644 was that between what we might call the victory party (who wanted to defeat the king decisively) and those who wished from an early stage to pursue peace (often people who had been close to the court before the war but who wanted to signal their opposition to the king's policies).

Following the spectacular parliamentary victory at the battle of Marston Moor (2 July 1644), for which the Eastern Association army under the command of the earl of Manchester was largely responsible, the earl seemed to lose faith in the need to win the war decisively. Oliver Cromwell, his lieutenant-general and an MP, increasingly bitter at the earl's failures, charged Manchester in the House of Commons with 'unwillingness ... to have this war prosecuted unto a full victory' (Abbott, 1938, vol. 1, p. 302). The divided command of an important part of parliament's military strength, the public row, and the antagonism between the two houses of parliament when Manchester invoked support from his fellow peers, did much to accelerate a measure that was to have far-reaching consequences – the Self-Denying Ordinance (which excluded from a seat in either house any soldier or office holder). This ideological division continued to affect the way in which parliament negotiated with the king and meant that there was a constant tension between those who wanted to end the war quickly, even though it meant accepting that the king retained a number of significant powers, and those who wanted to pursue the war to exact the maximum number of concessions from the king. It is important to remember, however, that it was not until late in 1648 that anyone really thought of doing without a king altogether.

A further difference between the two men was Manchester's support for the work of the Westminster Assembly of Divines and Cromwell's opposition to it. Those who wanted a church settlement as proposed by the Assembly to reform

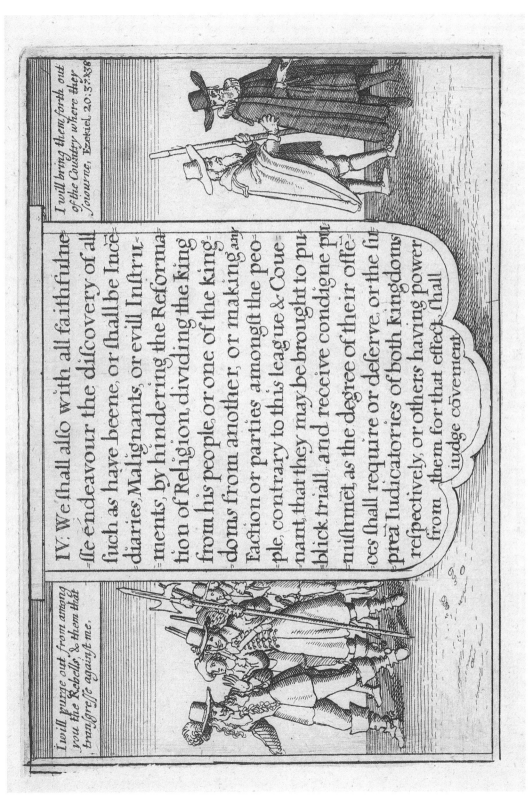

Figure 11.2 From *A Solemne League and Covenant for the Reformation and Defence of Religion, the honour and happinesse of the king, and the peace and safety of the three kingdoms of England, Scotland, and Ireland*, Edinburgh, Printed by Evan Tyler, 1643, p. 5. Photo: Huntington Library, California. Page showing left, the ungodly and, right, the godly.

the Church of England to bring it into conformity with Scotland's were known as Presbyterians. Their opponents (known as Independents) wanted a more devolved form of church organisation in which each congregation was paramount and which had no formal hierarchy of officers (such as bishops) or coercive powers (such as those exercised by the church courts). This difference emerged clearly in parliament, where Presbyterians (generally in favour of the Scots alliance) and Independents (generally opposed to it) began to act as separate interest groups. The Presbyterians formed a more cohesive group, more nearly resembling a modern political party, while the Independents were a looser alliance consistent with the kind of religious organisation they favoured.

Independents represented the emergence of a new kind of religious expression based on a multiplicity of individual congregations with an array of different religious beliefs. Lay people gathered round them communities of like-minded believers who tried out new forms of preaching and different kinds of belief unrestricted by the rules of the Church of England and the discipline and academic theology of the Anglican clergy. Increasingly, for such people a return to royal government, with all its associations of an established church with legal enforcement of practices and beliefs, was unthinkable. Although few people were prepared to admit that what they wanted was religious toleration, that was the effect.

Thomas Fairfax (1612–1671), a Yorkshire gentleman, served in the army of Sir Horace Vere in the 1620s. In 1642, he was appointed second in command of parliament's Northern Army, commanded by his father. In 1645, he was appointed by parliament commander-in-chief of the New Model Army, in which post he continued until 1650, when he resigned rather than invade Scotland. He lived quietly during the 1650s and was active in the moves to restore the king. He returned to private life after 1660.

Two developments promoted the spread of this religious heterodoxy. The first, as already suggested, was the lapsing of censorship of the press and pulpit. The second was the creation of the New Model Army in April 1645. This was formed out of several of the existing forces to provide parliament with a much more effective fighting force than it had hitherto had. It differed from the earlier armies in that its officers, though largely gentry and richer tradespeople, no longer included peers and MPs (with the exception of Oliver Cromwell).

The absence of censorship encouraged the emergence of radical Protestants, who had worshipped in secret in the 1630s or who had gone into exile. At the same time, there was a groundswell of support for these new religious forms, especially in the cities and in the New Model Army. Although the army was provided with chaplains – a mixture of Presbyterians and Independents – the feature that most commentators remarked on was the large number of laymen who preached and established religious meetings within their own regiments.

These laymen were influenced by Independents outside the army, and embraced a wide range of beliefs, some of which were regarded as heresy by orthodox Anglicans and Presbyterians. Figure 11.3 caricatures some of the more extreme beliefs – note the Anabaptist baptising someone by total immersion, the Libertine smashing the Ten Commandments, the naked Adamite and the Arminian (for Calvinist predestination had its radical as well as its Anglican critics).

In June 1645, 'the Royalist cause committed suicide' at the battle of Naseby (quoted in Woolrych, 2002, p. 316). Not only was this a crushing defeat, but letters captured from the king's baggage train made public Charles's negotiations with the Irish rebels. The victorious Cromwell, lieutenant-general to Fairfax, wrote to the speaker of the House of Commons saying:

> Honest men served you faithfully in this action, Sir, they are trusty;
> I beseech you in the name of God not to discourage them. ... He that
> ventures his life for the liberty of his country, I wish he trust God for
> the liberty of his conscience, and you for the liberty he fights for.
> (Quoted in Woolrych, 2002, p. 319)

His words reflect the growing distance between the army commanders and their civilian masters in parliament. Members of the army, mindful of the continued influence of the Scots, were concerned that parliament would negotiate a settlement with the king that would not justify to soldiers in the army the hardships they had undergone in the war.

In May 1646, following a series of military defeats by parliament, the king surrendered to the Scots army at Newark; in June, Oxford, headquarters of the royalist government, fell to parliament; and in July, negotiations for peace opened in Newcastle. While there was little chance that Charles would agree to swear the Solemn League and Covenant, the terms put to the king formed the basis for discussions for months to come.

Meanwhile, parliament debated what to do with its armies. By now, most soldiers were owed considerable arrears of pay, and there were some mutinies in provincial forces, but parliament decided in October 1646 to keep the New Model Army intact for another six months because it was known that the king was looking for armed assistance from abroad. Lands confiscated from the English bishops were used to raise £200,000 to pay off and send home the Scots army in February 1647. In return, the Scots handed over the king to parliament, who lodged him at Holdenby or Holmby House, Northants.

At the same time, parliament determined to try to solve the problem of Ireland, where the fighting had continued spasmodically since 1641, and to pay off as much of the army as possible. Exaggerated claims made about the radicalism of the New Model Army and pressure from the generally Presbyterian City of London (responsible for raising such funds as parliament could not find from taxation) persuaded parliament to send New Model Army soldiers to Ireland and to keep on foot in England provincial forces more sympathetic to Presbyterianism. When this plan became known, petitions began to circulate

Figure 11.3   *A Catalogue of the severall Sects and Opinions in England and other Nations, With a briefe Rehearsall of their false and dangerous Tenents*, London, printed by R.A., 1647. Photo: The British Library. Not all those pictured were heroes. The same lapsing of censorship that gave rise to a flourishing press also allowed freedom of religious expression. Many more conservative parliamentarians, especially those who were Presbyterian in religion, were horrified by the growth of what they regarded as heretical sects who took religious reform a step too far from the Anglican Church. Heresiographers (recorders of heresy) such as Thomas Edwards and Ephraim Pagitt sought to identify the enemy within. This broadsheet is loosely based on a longer work by Pagitt. You do not need to read the text below the image

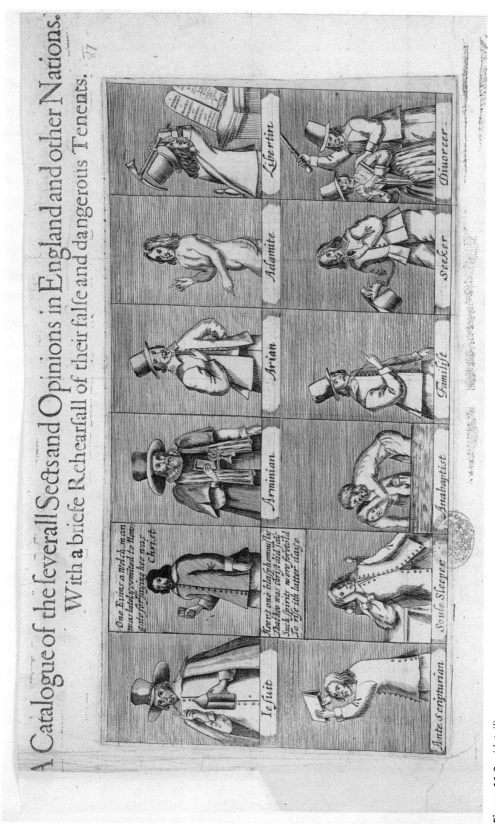

Figure 11.3   (detail)

within the army expressing the troops' concern about the payment of arrears, provision for indemnity against prosecution for acts committed in war, and their conditions of service in Ireland, especially given the uncertainty about who was to command the expedition. Delegates from parliament met an army council of forty-four New Model Army commanders in March; not one of the officers was prepared to serve in Ireland without satisfaction for their concerns. In a panic, parliament ordered the immediate disbanding of all forces except those destined for Ireland, while asserting that: 'all those who shall continue in their distempered condition, and go on advancing and promoting that petition, shall be looked upon and proceeded against as enemies of the State and disturbers of the public peace' (quoted in Gardiner, 1893, vol. 3, p. 229).

From restricting their demands to military matters, the soldiers moved on to political reform. This alteration in their temper, like the growth of religious radicalism, was influenced by developments outside the army, especially in London. A number of Londoners known as Levellers, mostly lesser gentry and tradesmen, some of whom had served in the army, began to articulate demands that there should be religious toleration, that supreme power should rest with the Commons, that all oaths and covenants (including the Solemn League and Covenant) be repealed and that the law be reformed. Their leaders, John Lilburne, William Walwyn and John Wildman, had published many pamphlets and began to form close links with the army petitioners.

In April 1647, cavalry regiments in the New Model Army elected representatives or 'agitators' (in the seventeenth century, the word agitator did not have the modern connotation of stirring up, the meaning was more akin to 'agent') and in May the infantry regiments did likewise. The two agents for each regiment felt able to make representations independently of the senior command of the army and made efforts not only to articulate their military grievances but to express views about the postwar world. In June, the army seized the king from Holmby House, transferring power from parliament to the army though, as Fairfax was at pains to assure parliament, they sought 'no alteration of the civil government' (quoted in Woolrych, 2002, p. 371). A general council of the army, consisting of over 100 officers and agitators from most regiments in the New Model Army, met at Reading in July to discuss a comprehensive scheme for settling the government of the kingdom that was presented to the gathering by Cromwell's son-in-law, Commissary-General Henry Ireton, and known as the *Heads of the Proposals*. It was intended that these should form the basis for negotiations with the king. Following a falling out with parliament and the City of London, Fairfax transferred the army headquarters to Putney, on the outskirts of the city. Here, debates about the *Heads of the Proposals* continued while the rank and file of the army, increasingly influenced by the Levellers, asserted that their commanders were acting against them rather than for them. A new statement of soldiers' demands, *An Agreement of the People*, was presented and debated at Putney by officers, agitators and civilian Levellers.

Read Anthology Document 3.13, 'Agitators and Levellers, 1647', extract (a), 'An Agreement of the People', and answer the following questions:

1   On whose behalf is the document presented?

2   By what right do the authors claim authority for the army to act?

3   What implications do the proposals have for the organisation of the state? (Think back to Table 9.1 in Unit 9.)

Spend about 10 minutes on this exercise.

1   It is presented by the agents of the five regiments of horse and then 'by the general approbation of the army'.

2   The authors use the device of saying that God, by delivering victory to them, has justified their initiative; they also claim that, because of the lack of 'frequent national meetings in council' (by which they mean parliament) and their ineffectualness, the former oppressions have not been removed.

3   Parliamentary constituencies would be reorganised to ensure a more equal distribution of population between each one. The electorate was the supreme power. An elected parliament alone had the power to legislate, to appoint judges, JPs and other officers of the judiciary and executive, to make war and peace, and to conduct foreign policy. All of this would have meant removing powers from the king and the House of Lords. There was to be no established church with coercive powers, no conscription (both sides in the war had conscripted soldiers from 1643), and no postwar prosecutions.

Although no one had proposed abolishing the monarchy, what was proposed was a state whose head had no legislative, judicial or executive power. It was also a state which, with religious toleration, had no religious justification for the right of the rulers to rule. Instead, the consent of the electorate was taken to provide that justification.

Read Anthology Document 3.13, 'Agitators and Levellers, 1647', extract (b), 'Extracts from the debates at Putney, 29 October 1647'. These extracts are not part of a continuous exchange between the participants but are representative of the views of the different groups. Answer the following questions:

1   What differences are there between Wildman's and Ireton's views?

2   How does Rainsborough characterise the views of the rank and file soldiery?

Spend about 10 minutes on this exercise.

1   Wildman appears to be arguing for a universal franchise on the basis of the free consent of the people, while Ireton (representing the senior officers of the army) appears to want a property qualification for electors, by which he means land rather than money.

2   Rainsborough asserts that the soldiers fought from conviction for their cause and that to insist on a property qualification for electors was to deceive the troops about the cause for which they had been fighting.

It is extraordinary that in five years, rank and file soldiers who, at the beginning of the war were starting to question the religious monopoly of the Church of England, were demanding constitutional reforms which implied what we would describe as a democratic republic. However, we need to beware of attributing too many modern thoughts to them. As with the English Peasants' Revolt (1381) that featured in Block 1, Unit 1, and the sixteenth-century German Peasants' Revolts (Block 2, Unit 6), aspirations of Levellers and soldiers reflected the condition of their own society. They did not envisage including women in the franchise and historians have discussed extensively whether they intended to allow servants to vote. Both women and servants were considered to be dependent on men (husbands, fathers, employers) who would represent the interests of their dependants. Leveller agitation in the army led to considerable discontent and to a widening breach between senior officers and soldiers, resulting in a number of courts martial for mutiny.

But while the army was debating the future, the king had escaped from the army's custody and was negotiating with the Scots. In December 1647, he concluded an Engagement with them under which he agreed to a limited implementation in England of the terms of the Solemn League and Covenant (see Anthology Document 3.14, 'Charles I's Engagement with the Scots, 1647'). In February 1648, the document became public, and war broke out in the spring with the Scots' occupation of Berwick and Carlisle and a rising in South Wales. A Scots army marched into England but was decisively defeated by the New Model Army at Preston in August. The Second Civil War, as this war was known, was a messy and violent affair and was accompanied by a rising in Scotland by extreme Covenanters who would have nothing to do with an uncovenanted king but who could not make common cause with the parliament's army, which they saw as filled with heretics. The king's Engagement with moderate Covenanters precipitated a split in Scotland that was to endure for decades to come.

Negotiations between parliamentary commissioners and the king opened at Newport on the Isle of Wight. The king made considerable concessions and agreement might conceivably have been reached with parliament but for the army, who believed that parliament was proposing to accept terms that would betray them. They removed the king from the Isle of Wight and marched on London. On 5 December 1648, parliament voted to continue to negotiate with the king and the following day a military force led by Colonel Pride ejected those members who had supported the vote (an event known as Pride's Purge). The remaining MPs, known as the Rump, voted to bring the king to trial before a specially constituted High Court of Justice on the capital charges of committing treason and levying war against his people.

Scotland and Ireland

For the Scots, the primary goal was to assure the preservation of a rightly reformed church; this justified alliances with whomsoever would best guarantee that. There had been a Scottish royalist army led by the charismatic general Montrose, but defeat at Philiphaugh in 1645 led to its disbanding in 1646. Meanwhile, the main Covenanting army served in England until paid off and sent home in 1647. Equally important had been the Scots commissioners in London, who worked with parliament and the Westminster Assembly of Divines to implement the terms of the Solemn League and Covenant. Their actions were directed from Scotland by the Scottish parliament (or, when it was not sitting, by the Committee of Estates) and by the General Assembly of the Kirk, whose primary interest was in securing a uniform religious settlement in a federalist polity. This agenda dominated Scots policy while being regarded as peripheral in England, for whom the alliance was much more one of 'political pragmatism and military expediency' (Macinnes, 1990, pp. 123–4).

Following the First Civil War, public offices in Scotland were purged of anyone tainted with royalism or who supported episcopacy; the Engagement brought back more moderate Covenanters (now known as Resolutioners) but the triumph of the radical Covenanters (now known as Protestors) was confirmed by their passing the Act of Classes on 23 January 1649. This gave the church a veto over office holders and ensured that anyone who had anything to do with the Engagement with Charles I was excluded from any position of power.

Following the outbreak of the rising in 1641, the Gaelic Irish rebels, arguing that they were fighting *for* the king, secured the support of a significant number of influential Old English, creating a single Catholic bloc. In October 1642, this Catholic alliance set up a provisional government in Kilkenny, which proclaimed its support for God, king and country, and in which Catholic clergy were an important presence. In 1643, a papal nuncio joined the confederation; the second of these, Giovanni Battista Rinuccini, who arrived in 1645, proved a formidable leader and counterweight to the Catholic noblemen who saw themselves as the leaders of the Confederation. Freedom of worship for Catholics in the areas controlled by the Confederation exposed Irish Catholics to continental Catholic influences, especially those of the Council of Trent, which had set about reforming European Catholicism in the wake of the Protestant Reformation (the set book by Wallace deals with this on pp. 124–6). The Confederates negotiated only with the royalists (since they regarded themselves as subjects of the king seeking recognition for their religion).

Supporters of parliament in Ireland were chiefly New English planters. Protestant regions of Ulster were controlled by Scots Presbyterians, reinforced by troops from Scotland under the command of George Munro, who cooperated uneasily with parliament's forces. The principal royalist leaders were the earl of Ormond, a Protestant Old Englishman, and the earl of Inchiquin, a member of the important Gaelic Irish O'Brien family who, from 1644 to 1648, changed his allegiance to parliament.

For the most part, the king regarded Ireland as a potential provider of troops in England while the English parliament (much influenced by the propaganda around the 1641 rising) regarded it as an uncomfortable neighbour who might harbour supporters of the king and thus needed subduing. Two expeditions were sent by parliament before 1649, but neither made much difference to the situation there.

Just as the divisions between the protagonists in Scotland related only partially to the divisions in England, so did those in Ireland. Just as the Covenanters established a kind of confessional state independent of the king, so, too, did the Catholic Confederation of Kilkenny. In both countries, wars were fought against England to preserve these gains.

Summary

It is clear that for many of those who took up arms in different parts of the British Isles, defence of religious beliefs and practices was paramount. For some, this included defending the religious justification for monarchy. Many combatants also believed fervently that God was on their side and viewed victories as signs of divine approval and defeats as signs of divine displeasure. But the course of the wars led to the evolution of new ideas both about religious liberty and about the nature of the state and the locus of power. The idea of a divine-right monarchy was irreparably damaged by events in all three nations.

Let us now look at the ways in which the population bore the cost of the wars.

THE COST OF THE WARS

Human cost

One of the most extraordinary aspects of the Civil Wars is how it was possible to sustain for so long wars where all sides needed to raise money, men and provisions. The cost in terms of lives lost as a result of military actions has been estimated at around 84,000 for England and Wales for the period 1642–51, of whom two-thirds died in the First Civil War (1642–46) (Woolrych, 2002, p. 335). Figures for Ireland are much more conjectural because the principal source is the 1641 depositions (see Unit 10). Disease – typhus, dysentery and the plague – accompanied armies and was rife in besieged cities, which accounted for further civilian deaths. While the armies roamed the country, wartime civilian mortality seems to have been relatively localised. In most southern counties in England, for example, the mortality rate in the period 1642–46 was level with that before and after the war; but Berkshire experienced a sharp and unrepeated rise in 1642–46, probably accounted for by the passage of armies along the Thames valley between London and Oxford. The Oxfordshire town of Thame also had a mortality crisis in 1643, probably caused by typhus brought by parliamentary forces arriving preparatory to an attack on Oxford (Bell, 1990, p. 144). The experience of Thame was repeated in other parishes close to military engagements, where civilian mortality rose, though the numbers of *military* burials recorded is insignificant (Dils, 1989, p. 49).

Civilian deaths and hardship were a major part of the human cost of the wars, with even children affected by the social upheaval and conflict. In order to piece together this 'history from below', and understand how large national and international events impacted on ordinary people, historians have needed to search out new, different sources, including accounts of individual experiences. Such sources are not numerous, not least because a substantial proportion of the population could not read or write. It is especially unusual to find an account by a woman. Frances King came from a prosperous clerical family, so was from the 'middling sort', as early modern historians often call the class of professionals (doctors, vicars, lawyers) and business owners (merchants, shopkeepers, etc.) – anyone who was neither labouring poor nor landholding gentry.

EXERCISE

Read Anthology Document 3.3, 'Mrs Frances King's account of the war and its aftermath', together with the headnote and footnotes, and then answer the following questions. The specimen answer provides fuller responses than you are expected to give after one reading, but do go back to the document a second time as you read the specimen answer to see for yourself how these have been arrived at.

1   What is the writer's background?

2   What can we learn from this document by implication (i.e. what can we learn from it beyond the facts the writer sets out to relate)?

3   What limitations does this have as a historical source (i.e. how far can we treat it as a strictly factual account)?

Spend about 60 minutes in total on this exercise

SPECIMEN ANSWER

1   The writer tells us that she was the daughter of a man called Dr John Manby, a clergyman who supported the king (lines 5, 13–14). She mentions her mother and her four siblings (lines 41–2, 57), with her personal information giving force to her account of the family's sufferings. She was born during the Civil Wars (she describes herself as a suckling infant) and the family was prosperous before they were targeted. Not only did her father have a living worth £500 a year, but her sister also had property. She went to school (line 104) where another child from a parliamentarian family ('son to an adversary') attacked her with a fork (probably a garden fork rather than cutlery).

2   Relating her father's qualifications, position and wealth is more than descriptive but part of setting out her credentials as a respectable and honest woman. Much of this story has been the subject of longstanding family discussions (lines 95–9), telling and retelling episodes so that they have acquired a kind of patina. The element of resolution in the tables being turned, from prosperity to poverty and back again on Charles II's Restoration, is part of a narrative technique, suggesting that, for all its stream-of-consciousness form, this is a tale that has been crafted. Her description of her father as a 'pious sufferer' for his treatment by parliamentarians (line 112) demonstrates that she regards the war as a religious as well as a political conflict.

3   On the face of it, this is an accurate account of the family's plight, full of vivid descriptions of events that were plainly told and retold among family and

friends with a great deal of circumstantial details. She was, after all, only a baby when many of these events happened, so they could only have been reported to her, not remembered personally.

DISCUSSION

In this account, as well as the family story, there is a clear impression of some of the effects of the war on people's day to day social relationships. Wright the sequestrator was despised for kowtowing to Cromwell (lines 84–6), and the fact that he and Talbot were both parishioners of her father seems to add to the sense of hurt. The children in the school playground had absorbed their parents' antipathy to royalists (lines 101–3). Note the irreverence of the woman who, asked in church to raise her hand if she supported Presbyterian church government, raised her foot (line 91).

However, there are reasons why we might want to retain an element of scepticism. First, most of the events described were not actually witnessed by the writer, but reported to her in later life. The letter itself has been written with a specific polemical purpose – to rehabilitate the reputation of Dr Manby and secure his inclusion in a memorial of royalist clergymen. There are both events and expressions that might give us some clues. Lines 54–7 tell us of Mrs Manby being searched by Wright, one of the sequestrators, and miscarrying as a result. Although this is a dreadful episode, very similar accounts appear in other letters written about the sufferings of royalist clergy and, more widely, in much writing about wartime atrocities through the ages.

In lines 112–114, the writer apologises for mistakes or errors in the writing. Now this letter, of more than 2,000 words in total (not all of it included here), has been written by someone who is fluent on paper and well accustomed to expressing herself in the written word. Such expressions of inadequacy are standard fare in women's writings of the period and in writing by a social inferior to a social superior.

Frances King's description of her parents' life during the civil war in England is unusual, the more so for being written by a woman. But, as you have seen, it is not a simple eye-witness account, it is a tale told for a particular purpose. That need not render the detail in it untrustworthy, but sources clearly need careful handling.

Let us now look at the experiences of two members of the gentry. Many literate people believed themselves to be living through extraordinary times and kept journals, describing the impact of civil war on their lives.

EXERCISE

Turn to Anthology Document 3.16, 'Passages from Isabella and Roger Twysden's diaries, 1645', and read extract (a), Isabella Twysden's journal.

1   What is the balance between recording public events and private matters?

2   What can a document such as this tell a historian of the Civil Wars?

Spend about 20 minutes on this exercise.

SPECIMEN ANSWER

1   The journal is a complete mixture of the personal and the public. It is difficult to tell which of the individuals she names Lady Twysden knew personally. She may have known Archbishop Laud, because as archbishop of Canterbury he lived in

Kent. The executions of the Hothams and Laud were nationally important events. Part of the purpose of the journal seems to have been to keep a record of the employment of the children's nurses and how much they were paid.

2   We learn something about the dissemination of news outside London and what events were considered to be significant (we do not know how Lady Twysden got to hear of what was happening in London – whether it was from letters, newsbooks or conversations with neighbours). Ordinary domestic life continued regardless of the war, but Lady Twysden had to take responsibility, in her husband's absence, for running the family's estate.

EXERCISE

Now turn to Anthology Document 3.16, 'Passages from Isabella and Roger Twysden's diaries, 1645', and read extract (b), Sir Roger Twysden's diary.

1   What do you notice about his wartime concerns?

2   Compare his writing and the content of his diary with that of his wife (both are in the original spelling)

Spend about 20 minutes on this exercise.

SPECIMEN ANSWER

1   Sir Roger was not directly involved in the fighting (at this time he was forty-eight years of age). His primary concerns were the welfare of his family: the birth of the child, his wife's travels, her need to get some payments from the estates and the attempt to get the fine reduced. While he was detained (under house arrest, rather than in prison), he pursued the antiquarian and legal interests common to many seventeenth-century gentlemen.

2   The spelling and expression are quite different. Though Sir Roger's spelling varies from modern spelling, it is consistent (for example, he writes 'knwe' instead of 'knew'). Isabella's is much more phonetic – it makes better sense if read aloud. The abbreviated form of Isabella's entries suggests someone without much time to spare and for whom penmanship may have been something of an effort, while Roger was plainly at ease with the written word.

DISCUSSION

By putting the two diaries together we learn a good deal more than either one of them can tell us on its own. We learn, for example, from Sir Roger's diary, that his wife dealt directly with the members of the parliamentary committee concerned with granting her an allowance.

We also see Sir Roger as a parliamentarian, not in the sense of a supporter of parliament in the war, but in the sense of someone who was a member of the political nation – a former MP who understood how parliamentary committees worked.

Note too, that the religious phraseology so commonly associated with supporters of parliament rises readily to his pen in his thanks for his wife's safe journey. This kind of language was shared by godly people on both sides of the divide over ceremonies and bishops.

Sir Roger Twysden's personal experience also provides historians with evidence of how the conflict impacted upon producers and consumers.

EXERCISE

Now read *Oxford Dictionary of National Biography* (*ODNB*), 'Sir Roger Twysden', in the Block 3 secondary sources on the A200 website – this is the *ODNB* entry on the life of Sir Roger. What was the financial cost of the civil war to him?

Spend about 20 minutes on this exercise.

SPECIMEN ANSWER

The City of London demanded £400 from him for their loan to parliament (he mentions this in his journal) despite being, as he argued, not a permanent resident of the city. His house contents were seized to meet this debt. His Kentish lands were sequestrated and the timber felled. To recover his lands he agreed to a fine of £3,000, which he could not afford to pay so the sequestration remained in effect. It was not until 1650 that he recovered his lands, having finally negotiated a fine of £1340 to recover them. In addition, he had to pay an assessment of £600, which was eventually reduced to £389 18s 6d.

DISCUSSION

Twysden was not an ardent royalist (he had refused to pay Ship Money), nor was he a particularly rich man. His annual income was assessed at £750, so the fines amounted to several years' income. He refused to join the king at Oxford in order to protect his family's property in Kent. However, his prewar career made him a notable figure and since his lands lay in a part of Kent that strongly supported parliament he had little chance of living out the war in obscurity. In addition to the forced loan and the fines, he was presumably charged with the monthly assessment tax and, like Frances King's family (Anthology Document 3.3), suffered at the hands of parliamentarian sequestrators.

Let us now expand the discussion on the producers and consumers theme and look at the costs of some of the forces that were maintained during the war.

Armed forces

Though the great set-piece battles had a significant impact on the politics of the period, such engagements were relatively unusual. All over England, but especially in the Midlands, were small garrisons, generally based on older fortified houses. These were usually manned by soldiers drawn from the surrounding area, who ventured out on skirmishes against forces from other similar garrisons. King and parliament developed similar systems of local administration to raise taxation, men and supplies. Parliament adopted the form of a weekly assessment levied on every £1 value of an individual's property, provided the property was worth more than £10. Local officials appointed by the parliamentary committee for the administration of each county collected and recorded the assessments. One of the Wiltshire collectors, based at Great Chalfield garrison, noted that 'the country had liberty to pay in victual, hay, oats, or might work it out at the fortifications; whereby far the greater part was brought in such provisions as they could spare' (Pafford, 1966 [1940], p. 45).

EXERCISE

You looked briefly at some churchwardens' accounts (Anthology Document 1.30(a)) in Unit 4, but you will now examine a statistical source more deeply. Look at Anthology Document 3.15, 'Supplying a provincial garrison', extracts (a) and (b), which are samples of the receipts and expenditure of the Great Chalfield garrison, and answer the following questions.

1   What do you notice about the goods, labour and money *collected* (shown in extract (a))?

2   What do you notice about the goods *bought* for the garrison (shown in extract (b))?

3   Can we conclude anything about the impact of such a garrison on the local community?

Spend about 10 minutes on this exercise.

SPECIMEN ANSWER

1   The greatest value was money (£21 16s), contrary to the collector's observation (above) that most people brought provisions. There was a large amount of cheese and grain (oats and wheat), and some malt. The arrears were surprisingly large – two-thirds of the total.

2   The disbursements for the garrison were for a miscellany of goods and services. There is no distinction between the wages bills (for the porter, the foot soldiers and the gunsmith), occasional payments for services (for work on the bulwarks, a guide, fetching Widow Somner's oxen, the spy and a messenger), military supplies (cannon and musket baskets, bridles) and domestic supplies (capons, butter, eggs, beer, earthenware and salt).

3   Providing food, clothing and equipment for 200 men and fodder for 100 horses was no small matter. Men and mounts were usually recruited locally for such garrisons, depleting the local labour force. In addition, residents of surrounding parishes had to find money, goods or labour to pay the assessment. But the garrison was also a paying consumer of local goods and services. It doesn't look as if it had to buy cheese or grain, but it was buying poultry and dairy products, and the amount of labour service it could call on was insufficient to do all the work needed on the fortifications so additional labourers had to be employed and paid.

DISCUSSION

1   Wiltshire was a county noted for cheese making and grain growing. The malt was used for making beer, the staple drink in the absence of safe water supplies. Only the poorest people tended to supply labour. The labour of the five men was calculated at 8d a day, the standard agricultural day-labourer's rate.

2   Many of the services the garrison required could probably be found locally; there were plenty of agricultural labourers. But gunsmithing was a skilled craft more usually associated with cities.

3   The assessment received at Great Chalfield was collected from about twenty-four parishes, including the market towns of Trowbridge, Melksham and Bradford-on-Avon, and fell far below the sums charged on each parish. There were few opportunities for local people to make large profits from providing goods and services to the garrison, but in other parts of the country manufacturing arms, ammunition and clothing for the army was of some importance. There were some seasonal variations: for example, in June, the garrison was buying peas, beans, kale, salad and radishes, and wheat, the earlier supplies having presumably been exhausted.

Local garrisons and forces relied on local supplies; New Model Army forces, which could number at least 17,000 men, were often quartered on local households. The larger armies passed repeatedly through the same areas of the country and householders must have found it difficult to provide food and animal fodder in the quantities required. Contractors in London seem to have been used to provide arms, clothing and equipment – at least £450,000 was spent on these in London between 1638 and 1652 (Coates, 2004, p. 90). There were also major contractors who manufactured and transported bulk quantities of cheese and biscuit (Nusbacher, 2000, pp. 155–9). Coates estimates that a high proportion of the £4.25 million spent on the New Model Army went into the London economy to buy food for the troops (Coates, 2004, p. 91). It is clear that contractors for food, clothing and equipment for the armies had some difficulty in getting paid. The sums involved could be very large – Stephen Estwick issued £23,000-worth of clothing to the earl of Essex's soldiers in 1642 and was still owed half that sum in April 1643 (Coates, 2004, p. 93).

Plainly the need to produce and transport such goods had an impact on the economy of London, but Ben Coates, historian of London's Civil War economy, concludes that while arms were imported and manufacturing capacity expanded there is little evidence for the development of more capitalistic modes of production (Coates, 2004, pp. 92, 100). Nor did new trade and financial networks and mechanisms need to be established; the London livery companies continued and developed their control of the trades with which they had traditionally been associated. Hence, there were winners as well as losers among producers and consumers in the economy of the Civil Wars.

ABOLISHING THE MONARCHY 1649

The trial and execution of the king

While there was fighting in progress, it is hard to discern the role of the state: had the state actually disintegrated? Think back to the functions of the state identified in Unit 9. The law courts had more or less collapsed and almost all the administration was directed to military matters, especially to the raising of taxes to pay the many armies. If we look at the qualities identified as being those of a state – a set of institutions with its own personnel, including the means of violence and coercion, and having the monopoly of rule making within that territory – we can see that these had multiplied. There were the institutions of the king's administration in Oxford; parliament's administration in Westminster and Whitehall; the Covenanting administration in Edinburgh; the Catholic Confederation of Kilkenny; and the remnants of the English administration in Dublin. All of these ran some of the institutions that characterise a state, and several of them (the king in Oxford, parliament in Westminster and the Confederation of Kilkenny) conducted extensive negotiations with foreign powers; the Confederation even had a papal nuncio in residence.

But the test of statehood came with the decision to put Charles I on trial. By what right could the victorious parliament of England put the king of England and Wales, Scotland and Ireland on trial? Remember (Unit 10, p. 52) that the Scots had already declared the king to be *under* the law, but there was no such convention in England. And in any case, what legitimacy had a House of

Commons originally elected in 1640 and reduced in membership from about 470 to around 200 MPs by Pride's Purge in December 1648? The House of Lords was now made up of only fifteen or so peers, of whom commonly fewer than ten sat to 'tell tales by the fireside in their House in the hope of more Lords to drive away the time' (quoted in Firth, 1910, p. 206). On 1 January 1649, the Commons, without a division, passed an ordinance to put the king on trial and appointed 150 commissioners (including six peers) to act as judge and jury. The following day, the ordinance was sent up to the Lords and was rejected by the twelve peers present.

EXERCISE

Look now at Anthology Document 3.17, 'The trial of Charles I, 1649', extract (c), 'Parliament and king, 27–30 January 1649'. What are the implications of the vote of 4 January 1649 that parliament on 30 January ordered to be printed?

Spend about 15 minutes on this exercise.

SPECIMEN ANSWER

The House of Commons declared that, as it represented the people of England who were 'the original of all just power', it had supreme power in the land and could by itself make laws without king or lords.

The Commons thus, on its own, set in train the arrangements for the king's trial.

EXERCISE

Read Anthology Document 3.17, 'The trial of Charles I, 1649', extract (a), 'Extracts from the trial proceedings'. What was the king's response to the charges made against him?

Spend about 15 minutes on this exercise.

SPECIMEN ANSWER

The king declined to answer the charges on the grounds that 'I would know by what power I am called hither', by what 'lawful authority'. Nevertheless, he attempted to debate with the court about the nature of his rights. He argued that he was a hereditary not an elective monarch, that he represented the people of England better than any High Court of Justice and that the Commons had no capacity as a law court.

DISCUSSION

The Commons, having already declared they were 'the supreme power in this nation', did not defend their actions. But they were scrupulous in procedural matters and collected depositions from witnesses to show the king's involvement in the war. There are two examples in Anthology Document 3.17, 'The trial of Charles I, 1649', extract (b), 'Depositions taken against the king', extracts (i) and (ii).

The court decided on the king's guilt and sentenced him to be executed; look back to the start of this unit for the impact of that occasion. Parliament had then to deal with the consequences of the vacancy of the head of state. It was (as it still is) customary for the new monarch to be proclaimed at the same time as the old one was declared dead. So, between 27 and 30 January 1649, prior to Charles I's death, the Commons passed an Act 'prohibiting the proclaiming any person to be king of England or Ireland, or the dominions thereof' and, to give it force, ordered that the Commons' claims of 4 January be printed (see Anthology Document 3.17(c)). In effect, this meant that the monarchy had been abolished: an Act confirming this was passed on 17 March and, on 6 February, the abolition of the Lords followed.

What became of the monarchy?

You will have noticed from Anthology Document 3.17(c) that the House of Commons at Westminster only declared on the prohibition of a king 'of England or Ireland'. Remember, that the English parliament had no jurisdiction over Scotland, even though they had shared the same king, so this ruling had no impact north of the border. In Scotland, Charles I's eldest son Charles was told he would be recognised as king on the condition of his 'espousing God's cause', and in 1651 he was crowned in Scotland by the marquis of Argyle (not, as would have been the case in England, by an ecclesiastic). After hearing a sermon, Charles swore the National Covenant and the Solemn League and Covenant. A Scottish observer noted that 'There were many bonfires set forth in token of joy. His majesty, when he was crowned, was not anointed at all, because the Commission of the Kirk thought it to savour somewhat of superstition' (Lamont, 1830, pp. 26–7). In Ireland, the leading royal servant, the earl of Ormond, had concluded a truce with the Catholic Confederation of Kilkenny in December 1648, and the Ulster Scots had agreed to put themselves under his command. Charles II was proclaimed king in Ireland in February 1649. However, after defeat at the battle of Worcester on 3 September 1651, Charles fled into exile on the Continent. He would not return to the British Isles for over eight years.

CONCLUSION

The Civil Wars had affected, in one way or another, all sections of the population and no one's life remained completely untouched. We have seen how the three module themes run through events. In terms of economics, taxation was increased as a direct outcome and troops might be billeted on families or garrisoned within communities with little recompense. For the thousands who fought, and the families who supported or rejected them for their decision, choices were hard – and could only have been made because of profound beliefs as to the prerogatives of the state not only over each subject's political life, but also over their immortal soul. With the 'peculiar and illogical combination of a difference of religions with a theory of authority in the king as supreme head of the church', a king presiding over multiple kingdoms, all of which were internally divided by faith, faced constant in-built challenges to his authority (Russell, 1987, p. 398). For a king like Charles I, pressing for greater uniformity within his state, the clash between his ideology and sense of his position as king and head of the Anglican church, and the beliefs of many of his subjects, was to prove disastrous.

The king was dead; the English parliament intended that there should be none to replace him, but the constitutional relationship between the Three Kingdoms meant that Scotland and Ireland could, in theory, agree or disagree with that judgement as they chose. Their shared king had been the common factor between them, politically; otherwise, in terms of the mechanics of governance – the legislature, judiciary, preferred confession, reach of state powers across communities – there were substantive differences. What, then, would keep them together in one state after Charles I's execution? Perversely, perhaps, parliamentarians would follow a similar path to the king they had rejected, in pressing for greater uniformity, and a closer union, between the Three Kingdoms. The English republic moved quickly to consolidate its position in the rest of the federated state by mounting conquest campaigns against Scotland and Ireland, and made several attempts to rework the entire constitutional framework of the state over the course of the 1650s.

REFERENCES

Abbott, W.C. (ed.) (1937) *The Writings and Speeches of Oliver Cromwell*, 4 vols, Oxford, Oxford University Press.

Bell, J. (1990) 'The mortality crisis in Thame and east Oxfordshire', *Oxfordshire Local History*, vol. 3, pp. 137–52.

Coates, B. (2004) *The Impact of the English Civil War on the Economy of London*, Aldershot, Ashgate.

Dils, J. (1989) 'Epidemics, mortality, and the Civil War in Berkshire 1642–6', *Southern History*, vol. 11, pp. 40–52.

Donegan, B. (2007) 'Varieties of royalism' in McElligott, J. and Smith, D.L. (eds) *Royalists and Royalism During the English Civil Wars*, Cambridge, Cambridge University Press, pp. 66–88.

Firth, C.H. (1910) *The House of Lords During the Civil War*, London, Longman.

Gardiner, S.R. (1893) *History of the Great Civil War*, new edn, 4 vols, London, Longman Green.

Gardiner, S.R. (1906 [1889]) *Constitutional Documents of the Puritan Revolution 1625–1660*, 3rd edn, Oxford, Clarendon Press.

Lamont, J. (1830) *The Diary of Mr John Lamont of Newton 1649–71*, Edinburgh, Maitland Club.

Macinnes, A. (1990) 'The Scottish constitution: the rise and fall of oligarchic centralism' in Morrill, J. (ed.) *The Scottish National Covenant in its British Context*, Edinburgh, Edinburgh University Press, pp. 106–33.

Memegalos, F.S. (2007) *George Goring (1608–1657): Caroline Courtier and Royalist General*, Aldershot, Ashgate.

Morrill, J.S. (1974) *Cheshire 1630–1660: County Government and Society During the English Revolution*, Oxford, Oxford University Press.

Morrill, J.S. (1976) *The Revolt of the Provinces*, London, George Allen and Unwin.

Nusbacher, A.J.S. (2000) 'Civil supply and the civil war: supply of victuals to the New Model Army on the Naseby campaign', *English Historical Review*, vol. 115, pp. 145–60.

Pafford, J.H.P. (ed.) (1966 [1940]) *Accounts of the Parliamentary Garrisons of Great Chalfield and Malmesbury 1645–46*, Devizes, Wiltshire Record Society, vol. 2.

Russell, C. (1987) 'The British problem and the English Civil War', *History*, vol. 72, pp. 395–415.

Russell, C. (1990) *The Causes of the English Civil War*, Oxford, Oxford University Press.

Vicars, J. (1644) *Jehovah Jireh. God in the Mount*, London.

Wedgwood, C.V. (1971 [1964]) *The Trial of Charles I*, London, Fontana.

Woolrych, A. (2002) *Britain in Revolution, 1625–1660*, Oxford, Oxford University Press.

Anne Laurence and Rachel C. Gibbons

INTRODUCTION

The execution of King Charles I on 30 January 1649 was a revolutionary event in many ways. However, it did not prove to be the end either of the Civil Wars or of the monarchy in the British Isles; instead, it was the start of a process of constitutional experiment and negotiation that would continue for the remainder of the seventeenth century and beyond. In the same way that, earlier in the block, we explored what came *before* the Civil Wars (their origins and context, including their place within a broader European picture), it is important that we also consider what came *after*, in order to understand them more fully and acquire a clearer perspective of their impact. Therefore, this unit will look forwards, across the constitutional experiments of the Commonwealth, the Restoration (1660) and what is most commonly known as the Glorious Revolution of 1689.

Given the constraints of one week's work, this unit couldn't be (and isn't intended to be) a complete history of the second half of the seventeenth century. Its main purpose is to explore the consequences of the post-Civil Wars political settlement, and how parliament attempted to frame a new constitution – first, around the vacuum left by the removal of the king and, then, to remake the monarchical role within government. The main theme, then, is state formation and a renegotiation of relations between the three kingdoms. If the start of this period is symbolised by the death of Charles I, the symbolic moments that punctuate and redirect it are two royal landings: that of King Charles II (*1660–1685) at Dover on 23 May 1660, and that of William of Orange (who would become King William III) at Torbay on 5 November 1688. These two events signify the fundamental change that had taken place as a result of the Civil Wars – that kings were seen to rule only by the consent of their subjects (a fact acknowledged by the kings themselves). They represent both that Charles and William were invited to come, and also that two kings, Charles I and James II, had been removed, the former by execution and the latter by his flight.

As with the decision to remove, and then execute, Charles I, these invitations to reign originated with the parliament of England; it was down to Scotland and Ireland to go along with those decisions on their own terms, or not, as they chose. Charles II had been declared king of Scotland and Ireland within days of his father's execution, and crowned in Scotland in 1651, so the 1660 Restoration was a case of England catching up with the other two kingdoms. The landings of 1660 and 1688 were essentially English moments, and the events that one might choose to define the transition from one regime to another in the histories of Scotland and Ireland could be different, and represent the more troubled post-Civil Wars histories of those countries.

Figure 12.1   William III on horseback, late seventeenth century, English delftware, 7.6 x 35.5 cm. Fitzwilliam Museum, Cambridge. Photo: Fitzwilliam Museum, Cambridge. Depictions of the victorious Protestant William appeared in many guises. One of the most popular was on painted Delftware pottery, the fashion for which came from the Netherlands. This image was reproduced frequently on large dishes. It was transposed and adapted from an engraving by Cornelis van Dalen of Charles I entering Edinburgh

Charles II (*1660–1685) was declared king in Scotland and Ireland when his father was executed in 1649. He was invited to return to England as monarch in 1660 and resumed the kingship of all three kingdoms. His heir was his Catholic brother James. Charles vigorously opposed a plan to upset the hereditary succession by installing his illegitimate but Protestant son James, duke of Monmouth, as heir instead.

In Scotland, William and Mary were proclaimed king and queen on 11 April 1689, but it was perhaps the massacre of thirty-eight Highlanders at Glencoe on 13 February 1692 that defined the difficulty William had in subduing Scotland, not merely because of Highlanders' continued support for the departed King James, but also because of endemic feuding and regional rivalries within the kingdom.

In Ireland, which James used as his base for trying to recover his throne, the defining moment might be the battle of the Boyne (1 July 1690), commemorated in many images of William (see Figure 12.1). Another episode that similarly resonates, year after year, in the public display of Northern Ireland is the siege of Derry. The gates of the city were barred against James's Catholic forces by thirteen apprentice boys on 7 December 1688. The siege of the city began in April 1689 and lasted 105 days. A counterpart event within the Catholic community, the defence of Limerick against William's army in the First Siege, is celebrated in a traditional dance. The Second Siege of Limerick ended in the city's surrender and the signing of a treaty on 3 October 1691, offering terms to James's supporters (Jacobites) remaining in Ireland and allowing the besieged army to leave for France. 14,000 soldiers, with around 10,000 women and children, went into exile in what is popularly known as the 'Flight of the Wild Geese' – an event widely taken to mark the end of the Williamite War in Ireland.

This unit explores administration under the Commonwealth (1649–60) and the consequences of the Restoration. Additionally, it will consider why it was that some of those matters unresolved in 1660 could not be settled until James II (VII in Scotland) had departed and William (*1688–1702) and Mary (*1688–1694) were installed as monarchs, and why William's arrival in 1688 was greeted in a rather more muted fashion than that of Charles II. In the course of this unit, we will look at:

- the different forms of government tried during the Commonwealth period
- how the restoration of the monarchy was put into effect
- how opposition developed under Charles II and James II
- the nature and extent of the Glorious Revolution
- changes in the constitution of the state made up by the three kingdoms over the second half of the seventeenth century

- how historians can use statistics and how they can manipulate them through a spreadsheet, using the example of the ecclesiastical census of 1676 known as the Compton Census.

The interrelationship of England (with Wales), Scotland and Ireland in this period, first as part of a unitary Commonwealth and then, after 1660, as again three separately governed kingdoms within one state with a king at its head, remains vital to understanding events of the time. 'It is in a British, not an English, context that the true importance of the Interregnum and Restoration should be appreciated', stresses Ronald Hutton. He also argues that, just because it was short-lived, we should not dismiss the Commonwealth merely as a failed experiment – 'it is not too much of an exaggeration to suggest that during the years 1649–53 the modern political relationships of the three realms were formed' (Hutton, 1990, p. 135).

Constitutional change comes mainly under the theme of state formation but, of course, we must also consider the importance of political beliefs and ideologies in dictating the workings of that state and acceptance (or not) of the king at its head. Religious beliefs and ideologies, and the difficulties of multiple confessions within a federated state with an established church, continue to drive conflict in this latter half of the seventeenth century – and end up being the deciding factor in whether a king is acceptable or not to the majority of his subjects. Discussion of both these themes across the block, and of broad consequences of events on producers and consumers, will feature in the Conclusion to Block 3.

THE COMMONWEALTH 1649–60

The constitution and the three kingdoms

For this section you will find it helpful to consult Table 12.1, later in this unit. During the years 1649–60, different experiments in government were tried. One of the most novel features was the introduction of a written constitution, unlike the ancient unwritten constitution of king in parliament. Another was the creation of a parliamentary union of England and Wales, Scotland and Ireland, something that was not subsequently achieved until the Acts of Union of 1800.

The first written constitution, the Instrument of Government, was drawn up by General John Lambert and approved by the Council of Officers in December 1653; it vested power in a protector (Oliver Cromwell) and a Council of State, of between thirteen and twenty-one members to be chosen from names put forward by parliament, whose actions parliament could veto. The protector had the power only to hold up legislation for twenty days; he had no power to veto it. The Humble Petition and Advice of 1657 was drawn up by a group of civilians and was intended to correct problems that had arisen in the implementation of the Instrument of Government and the troubles of the first two Protectorate parliaments. It introduced a new second chamber (to replace the dissolved House of Lords) alongside the Commons – a senate of nominated worthies. It increased the protector's powers over the council; it much increased the government's income; and it considerably limited the *de facto* religious toleration of the Instrument of Government. It also invited Cromwell to assume the title of king (but not hereditary monarch) and to nominate his successor. He declined the first and did not avail himself of the second until September 1658, when he was dying. While the constitutions contained many reforming measures, they failed to secure the support of the political nation and thus linked the Protectorate to the fortunes of the army.

During the administration of the Rump Parliament, some discussions about parliamentary union with Scotland took place, and (as you can see from Anthology Document 3.18, 'Scotland under the Commonwealth', extract (b), 'The diary of John Lamont, 1652') the union was declared in 1652, but its first realisation was with Barebone's Parliament (1653). Its four Scots members were not dyed-in-the-wool Covenanters: they needed to have some sympathy with the prevailing Independent religious views of the majority of English members. The six Irish members were neither Irish nor religious radicals, but represented Protestant settlers and soldiers in Ireland. A union between England and Scotland was only formally enacted in 1657, and then without a proper form of assent by the Scottish people. In the three Protectorate parliaments (1654–59), the Scots were under-represented, there being four hundred English MPs and thirty Scots, leading a Scot to comment that the relationship was 'as when a poor bird is embodied into the hawk that hath eaten it up' (quoted in Donaldson, 1978 [1965], p. 344). In contrast, no act of union between England and Ireland was passed and English authority over Ireland was exercised by the protector and Council of State rather than through the army officers who made up most of Ireland's thirty MPs in Protectorate parliaments.

Underlying the constitutional experiments was the army. It was the military who governed the sitting and dissolution of assemblies. When, in 1653, Cromwell dissolved the Rump parliament, he did so with the support of the Council of Officers who proposed the scheme for an assembly whose 144 members (including four for Scotland and six for Ireland) were to be nominated from among religious congregations. This parliament is known by the name of a London member, Praise-God Barebone. Before Barebone's Parliament met, Cromwell simply governed as commander-in-chief of the army. The military were behind the Instrument of Government (1653). They protested against the intentions of the Humble Petition and Advice (1657) to increase civilian control, and caused Richard Cromwell to dissolve his parliament (1659). They recalled and expelled the Rump Parliament; then, General Monck, arriving from his command in Scotland, recalled to it the MPs who had been excluded by Pride's Purge in 1648, and opened negotiations with the exiled Charles II.

The state and the military

Two particular features of the period illustrate the dependence of the Commonwealth state on the army. The first was the military occupations of Scotland and Ireland throughout the period and the second was what is known as the 'rule of the major-generals' (October 1655 – January 1657).

Following the invasion of Scotland in 1650 and the defeat of the Scots by the New Model Army at Dunbar and Worcester, a military government was established in Scotland with a number of garrisons which were maintained until 1660, even though the administration was increasingly handed over to civilians. One particular consequence of the occupation was the idea that Scottish legal procedures should be assimilated with those of England (though for some time it was martial law that ruled).

EXERCISE

Read Anthology Document 3.18, 'Scotland under the Commonwealth', extract (a), 'The diary of John Nicoll, December 1651', and extract (b), 'The diary of John Lamont, 1652'.

What elements of the English occupation do the two men highlight?

Spend about 15 minutes on this exercise

SPECIMEN ANSWER

Nicoll noted the abolition of the Scottish courts and his comments suggest that the religious practices of the soldiers were only made tolerable by their good discipline. Lamont noted the proclamation of the union without consultation and the abolition of the Scottish courts.

In Ireland, the suppression of resistance to the English parliamentary forces was more protracted, with an army led initially by Oliver Cromwell embarking on (essentially) a war of conquest in 1649. Ireland was seen as a serious problem to the new Commonwealth because of the danger posed, in the aftermath of the king's execution, by the uniting of two hitherto separate opponents of the parliamentarians, the Irish Catholic Confederation of Kilkenny and the royalists led by Ormond. Cromwell's own campaign in Ireland lasted from July 1649 until May 1650, the most infamous engagements of which were the destruction of Drogheda and of Wexford. Was Cromwell's brutal and intolerant attitude in Ireland – a stark contrast to his aspirations for tolerance and rapprochement in Scotland and England – evidence that he had 'swallowed whole the horror stories of Irish atrocities' that flooded England in pamphlets in 1641–42 after the rising (Coward, 2003 [1980], p. 249) (Unit 10, p. 57 and Figure 10.8)? If so, this is strong evidence of the power of propaganda in altering attitudes and behaviours in what was an already unpleasant conflict between neighbours. Though an administration was established in Dublin, it was 1652 before the country could be considered subdued, and the military aspect of England's direct government remained much more obvious in Ireland than in Scotland. There were over 20,000 parliamentarian soldiers there in 1654, and even in 1658 there were 12,000.

State and army became even more synonymous in the two-year phase of quasi-military rule in England under the major-generals. After the failure of the Protectorate parliament to agree on the terms of the Instrument of Government and a failed royalist rebellion, Penruddock's Rising, in March 1655, the Council of State decided to appoint regional military governors known as major-generals. England and Wales were divided into twelve districts, in which each major-general had powers to raise and direct new county militias to maintain peace and security, and to pay for them by levying a new tax on royalists, even those who had been quiescent, who possessed land worth £100 per annum or who had £1,500-worth or more of personal assets. This militarisation of the government of England and Wales did not involve large numbers of soldiers; indeed the government had been trying since 1653 to reduce the size (and cost) of the army and had already disbanded a significant number of soldiers. But it meant government by military officers in their capacity as members of the army rather than simply as agents of parliament. It was the most hated feature of the government of the Protectorate and major-generals were reviled as tyrants.

EXERCISE

Read Anthology Document 3.19, 'The rule of the Major-Generals, 1655–7', which consists of letters from Major-General Thomas Kelsey. What were Kelsey's greatest concerns?

Spend about 15 minutes on this exercise.

SPECIMEN ANSWER

In the first letter, Kelsey's concerns were with chasing up and disarming former royalists ('delinquents' and 'malignants'), understandable in the light of Penruddock's Rising, and with raising planned taxes. In the second, his concerns were with the blasphemous statements of Richard Coppin and their influence on the troops at Rochester. He also shows some concern for the public reputation of the administration, wanting to avoid slurs of persecution.

DISCUSSION

Kelsey's letters reflect the preoccupations of the Protectorate government in these years, both the major-generals and parliament – namely, royalist plots and public morality. This was also the period when parliament approved several measures aimed at imposing a Puritan moral code. Public entertainments such as theatres, cock-fighting and bear-baiting – anywhere where royalists might secretly assemble without attracting attention – were restricted, while religious holidays were stripped of many well-loved traditions seen as holding any possible 'papist' or pre-Christian connotation.

The rule of the major-generals brought to a head the uneasy relations between civilians and the military in the government. But removing the major-generals in 1657 did not solve any problems. One of the features of the 1650s was that anyone contemplating a restoration of civilian rule was conscious of the army waiting on the sidelines, and knew that without the army they could not govern. The final test came in 1658, when Cromwell died. Although there was little change in the personnel of the administration, we might have expected a further advance towards civilian rule with a new protector. Richard Cromwell, Oliver's eldest surviving son, was not a military man but the army forced him to dissolve his parliament of 1659. Thereafter, the calling and dissolving of assemblies was in the hands of the army and, ultimately, those of General Monck, with whom Charles II was in correspondence in March 1660 before his return.

Reprise

Treating the Civil Wars, the removal of the king and the different regimes of the Commonwealth as stages of one political story, now spend some time reading through Table 12.1, which summarises the changes to the state that took place over the period 1642–60. You don't need to learn details by heart but you should use the table as an aid to understanding the scale and the scope of the changes that took place over a relatively short period of time. At the end of the unit, there will be an opportunity to reflect in a similar way on the period 1660–91.

In this table, you can see, for example, how a good many of the functions of the state existed in parallel until the early 1650s, when the parliamentarians created a single polity, though not one with a uniform judiciary, church or local administration. You recall from Unit 9 (p. 13) that Conrad Russell described Charles I's position as 'head of a multiple monarchy' (Russell, 2000 [1987], p. 82). Likewise, the state over which Cromwell and the Council of State presided was not a unitary state, but a multiple one. However, while Russell attributes the breakdown of relations between the king and his subjects to Charles's attempts to impose uniformity on his kingdoms, it seems that the collapse of the Protectorate, of the republic, owed more to tensions between civilians and the military – to a crisis of legitimacy, and disagreements about who should exercise control, rather than to a failure of political processes.

The most striking feature of the years 1649–60 was that there existed a *de facto* republic even though Scotland and Ireland had not abolished the monarchy. In the course of the 1640s, there emerged a strain of republican thinking, often allied to radical Protestantism, but confessed republicanism was unusual and viewed with suspicion by many in the Protectorate government, including Oliver Cromwell. It is striking, in fact, how rapidly objections to monarchical rule melted away with the prospect of a return to political stability under the fresh face of Charles II.

Table 12.1   Changes in the state 1642–60

	England and Wales	Scotland	Ireland
Ruler	King Charles I until 30 January 1649. Oliver Cromwell, lord protector, December 1653 to September 1658. Richard Cromwell, lord protector, September 1658 to 1659. Council of State 1660.	King Charles I until 30 January 1649. Charles II declared king in 1649 and crowned in 1651, but in exile from 1651. Role of head of state occupied by whoever was head of state in England 1651–60.	King Charles I until 30 January 1649. Charles II declared king in February 1649. Role of head of state occupied by whoever was head of state in England 1649–60, but no formal act of union was passed.
Legislature	House of Commons, 1640–53 (c.470 MPs; purged of c.200 MPs in 1648, known thereafter as the Rump). House of Lords, 1640–1649 (when abolished).	Scottish parliament (estates), 1636–41, 1644–47 (after 1640 met without royal authority). Bishops excluded from 1639. In the absence of the estates sitting, business was conducted by the Committee of Estates replacing the Committee of the Lords of the Articles. Membership in 1641 was 56 nobles, 50 gentry and 54 burgesses.	Irish Parliament (240 MPs, of whom 20% were Catholic before the rising of 1641), last sat in 1642 but was continued by prorogations until 1646. General Assembly of the Confederation of Kilkenny, 1642–49, controlled Catholic Ireland (9 meetings; c.250 members representing the same constituencies at the parliament, Catholic bishops, c.19 Catholic peers).
	Barebone's Parliament, July to December 1653 (134 MPs for England and Wales).	Barebone's Parliament, July to December 1653 (4 MPs for Scotland).	Barebone's Parliament, July to December 1653 (6 MPs for Ireland).
	1st Protectorate parliament, September 1654 to January 1655 (400 MPs for England and Wales).	1st Protectorate parliament, September 1654 to January 1655 (30 MPs for Scotland).	1st Protectorate parliament, September 1654 to January 1655 (30 MPs for Ireland, most of whom were army officers).
	2nd Protectorate parliament, September 1656 to February 1658. 3rd Protectorate parliament, January to April 1659. Elected on a franchise of all adult males with real or personal estate valued at £200 except Catholics, abettors of the Irish rebellion. Rump Parliament, May to October 1659. 2nd recall of Rump, December 1659. Commons including members excluded in 1648, February to March 1660.	2nd Protectorate parliament, September 1656 to February 1658. 3rd Protectorate parliament, January to April 1659.	2nd Protectorate parliament, September 1656 to February 1658. 3rd Protectorate parliament, January to April 1659.

Judiciary	Judges were appointed under the Great Seal of the Commonwealth. Church courts abolished 1646, regulatory functions taken over by JPs. Judicial functions of House of Lords lapsed with its abolition in 1649. Attempts made to reform courts, especially Chancery.	Court of Session lapsed in July 1651. Justice temporarily in hands of a committee of English army officers. May 1652, 8 commissioners of justice installed (5 English and 3 Scots). Heritable jurisdictions and baron courts (feudal courts) replaced by JPs. Senior judges by mid 1650s were mainly Scotsmen.	After 1649, only Protestants could practise in the law courts. Common law courts were revived after the war but senior legal officers were usually Englishmen.
Executive	Royal Privy Council in Oxford until 1646. Parliamentary Committee of Safety, 1642–43; Committee of Both Kingdoms (with Scots members), 1644–47; Derby House Committee, 1647–49; Various Councils of State, 1649–60. Parliamentary organisation of county committees extended into peacetime. 1655–57, Major-Generals for each county.	Privy Council lapsed July 1651 with collapse of royalists. Covenanters' business was carried out by Committee of Estates and subcommittees, 1643–51. Some overlap in membership with Kirk's commission for public affairs. October 1651 to July 1655, government conducted by 8 English military commissioners. July 1655, Council of State of 8 members.	Royal administration in Dublin, 1642–49. Ormond lord lieutenant, 1643–60 (in exile 1650–60). Lord Lisle appointed lord lieutenant by parliament, 1646–47. Supreme council of the Confederation of Kilkenny over Catholic Ireland, 1642–49 (c.24 members). May 1650 to November 1651, Henry Ireton commander-in-chief; November 1651, Edmund Ludlow commander-in-chief; July 1655, Henry Cromwell commander-in-chief; November 1657, Henry Cromwell lord deputy; October 1658, Henry Cromwell lord lieutenant; June 1659, Cromwell replaced by English parliamentary commissioners; July 1659, Edmund Ludlow commander-in-chief; December 1659, Council of Officers assumed control.
Foreign policy	During the war, directed both from London and from Oxford. From 1649, directed by Council of State and protector in Whitehall. Foreign states began to recognise the new regime and to send ambassadors to London, despite the embarrassment of a royal court in exile.	Directed from Whitehall.	Directed from Whitehall. Confederation of Kilkenny, 1642–49, had papal nuncio in attendance and negotiated with foreign Catholic powers.

Defence	Royal Council of War in Oxford; field army; local forces under Commissions of Array and parish officers. Some forces from Ireland (mainly English settlers). Parliament's field armies; local forces at first under lords lieutenant and deputy lieutenants, later under county committees. From April 1645, field armies and some local forces combined into the New Model Army under the command of Sir Thomas Fairfax. Locally raised armies continued to outnumber the New Model Army until 1648.	Covenanting army led by Leslie and Callandar. Royalist army led by Montrose, 1643–46. After 1651, army of occupation controlled from Westminster and based on 5 principal Scottish forts. 18,000 soldiers in 1654 reduced to establishment of 10,500 by 1657.	Forces commanded by English administration at Dublin Castle; some raised by noblemen for king; forces of Confederation of Kilkenny; forces from Scotland commanded by George Munro; forces sent by parliament. After 1650, army directed from Dublin Castle by advisers from Westminster. 34,000 men in 1652, 23,000 in 1654, around 16,000 from 1655.
Taxation	Levied from areas occupied by royalists and parliamentarians during wartime. Instrument of Government, 1653, provided for revenue sufficient to support army of 30,000 men, a fleet and £200,000 per annum to support civil government, all other needs to be funded by parliamentary vote.	Monthly assessment on real and personal estate; did not support costs of administration and army.	Military supported by payments from England.
Church	Westminster Assembly of Divines appointed in 1643 to produce new church settlement to conform to Solemn League and Covenant. Presbyterian system partially implemented. Partial system of Presbyterian assemblies set up. Use of Anglican services and Prayer Book proscribed. From 1649, freedom of conscience except for Catholics and Anglicans, but exponents of extreme views (such as denying the divinity of Christ or flouting all God's laws) prosecuted. Proposal to abolish tithes not enacted.	General Assembly of the Kirk until 1653, when dissolved because it had no authority from new parliament in London. Military administration in favour of toleration of most forms of Protestantism. Some radical sects established by English soldiers. Protestors (radical Covenanters) in sympathy with military occupation, but Resolutioners (who had supported Engagement) more numerous.	Protestant church administered by secular administration in Dublin, main efforts addressed to English garrisons; some Church of Scotland congregations. Catholic priests to be executed under Act for Settling Ireland 1652. Catholic Ireland administered by Catholic bishops during period of Confederation of Kilkenny, 1642–49, with intervention from papal nuncio.

WHAT WAS RESTORED IN 1660?

On the face of it, the decision to invite Charles II to return solved the problem of who governed the country. No longer was there a contest between the military and parliament as to who controlled the head of state. Now there was a head of state who would technically rule 'in parliament' and who would be responsible for summoning the military in case of national danger. Abraham Cowley's verse extravagantly celebrated the king's arrival:

> All England but one bonfire seems to be,
> One Etna shooting flames into the sea.
>> *Ode Upon His Majesties Restoration and Return*

While the diarist John Evelyn wrote on 3 May 1660 'Praised be for ever the Lord of Heaven, who only doeth wondrous things, because his mercy endureth for ever' (Evelyn, n.d., p. 321). But, welcome as Charles II was, many vital matters were left unresolved. What was most pressing differed from kingdom to kingdom. In England and Scotland, it was the church; in Ireland, it was land. In all three kingdoms, the relations of the monarch with parliament were ill defined and the extent of his extra-parliamentary powers was unclear.

Charles II was invited to return by a group of English notables; the Scots and the Irish were not consulted about the Restoration, and it was the support of the English military (the army in Scotland commanded by General George Monck) that assured Charles II's arrival. The trial and execution of Charles I, and the parliamentary dissolution of the monarchy that followed in 1649, was exclusively an English project – and so was the Restoration eleven years later. After the dissolution of the Rump in March 1660, a convention was summoned (known as a convention because it had called itself; it had not been summoned by the king). It was elected on the franchise used for the Long Parliament, rather than that used for the Protectorate parliaments, and thus contained only representatives for England and Wales. Before it met, Charles II issued what is now known as the Declaration of Breda.

EXERCISE	Read Anthology Document 3.20, 'Extract from the Declaration of Breda, 4 April 1660'. What powers did Charles claim for himself and what did he leave to parliament?

Spend about 20 minutes on this exercise.

SPECIMEN ANSWER	Charles referred to himself as 'defender of the faith', which implies that he regarded himself as head of the Church of England, and to the 'restoration' of 'king, peers and people to their just, ancient and fundamental rights'. He claimed the right to issue a general pardon. He also claimed the right to allow 'liberty to tender consciences', implying religious toleration.

This skilful document left to parliament decisions that were bound to be controversial: the extent of liberty to tender consciences; title to land bought or otherwise acquired during the 1640s and 1650s; and the payment of the army.

Meanwhile, the executive in London continued to rule Scotland and Ireland. The Restoration in Scotland began properly when the king nominated members to a Scots Privy Council (many of whom were Covenanters who had redeemed themselves by supporting the Engagement with Charles I in 1647 or by their opposition to the invading parliamentary forces in 1650–51). The Scottish estates, nobles and representatives of the burghs, did not meet until January 1661 to legislate for the new dispensation. The equivalent to the king appointing members of the Scots Privy Council was in Ireland the appointment of lords justices and a lord lieutenant (General Monck) and deputy; the Irish parliament met in May 1661.

England and Wales

We talk about the *restoration* of the monarchy in 1660 but, apart from Charles II returning from exile, to what extent was pre-Civil-War society reinstated? This certainly seems to have been an aspiration of the restored monarchy – to treat the Commonwealth years merely as an interregnum between two Stuart kings, to be confronted, yes, but then smoothed over as much as possible. The House of Commons was restored on the old franchise and the House of Lords reassembled with bishops. All legislation passed after 1641 was declared null and void: everything that had had Charles I's assent was retained, notably the statutes that righted the most pressing grievances of the eleven years' personal rule, such as the abolition of the prerogative courts, feudal dues and prerogative taxes such as Ship Money. The most significant new regulation was the 1664 Triennial Act, which required parliament to meet every three years but not necessarily that a new parliament be called.

Many loyal royalists hoped that there would be some material restitution for their losses, but pragmatism ruled the day. In England, royalists who had forfeited their estates received compensation, while those who had sold their estates to pay fines (the majority) were not. Many royalists were in a similar situation to that of Sir Roger Twysden, of having had to pay swingeing fines rather than having their estates expropriated. The lands of the king, bishops, and deans and chapters that had been confiscated, sold and used to fund the Commonwealth were restored to their previous owners, the royal lands yielding an income of about £100,000 a year.

While only the regicides, those responsible for the 1641 rebellion in Ireland and a few other individuals were exempted from a general pardon, former supporters of parliament were justified in thinking that it was on the subject of religion that the king's supporters exacted their revenge. Despite Charles II's wishes, as expressed in the Declaration of Breda before his return, the parliament that met in 1661 and was finally dissolved in 1678 passed a succession of laws (known as the Clarendon Code) against Protestant nonconformity. In 1662, all clergy were required to assent to the new Book of Common Prayer (including the Thirty-Nine Articles) with the result that some 2,000 ministers felt forced to resign their livings. These ministers were banned from preaching or living within five miles of their old parishes.

Meetings for religious worship outside the established church were prohibited and anyone refusing to take the oath of allegiance was excluded from municipal corporations.

Scotland

> The application of the term 'restoration' to the period after 1660 misrepresents the nature of Scottish political and ecclesiastical life in those years. The monarchy was restored and the machinery of government in parliament, privy council and the judicature was again much as it had been before the outbreak of the covenanting revolt. But behind these externals, many essentials were different from what they had been under Charles I, and in so far as the revolt against that monarch had been aristocratic and anti-clerical it found its fulfilment rather than its negation under Charles II.
>
> (Donaldson, 1978 [1965], p. 358)

Donaldson's summary of the effect of the Restoration suggests that, for the Scots, a simple return to the status quo of the 1630s would not suffice. Though bishops were restored to the Church of Scotland, the general policy was to reinstate the church as it had been under King James VI and I, rather than as it had become under King Charles. While this was acceptable to many Scots, to the radical wing of the Covenanters, especially strong in south-west Scotland, who abhorred the Engagement with Charles I, it confirmed their alienation and some 270 ministers left the Church of Scotland rather than acknowledge bishops and repudiate the covenants.

A nostalgic Covenanting minister wrote of the time up to the Restoration:

> At the king's return every parish had a minister, every village had a school, every family almost had a Bible, yes, in most of the country all the children of age could read the scriptures ... I have lived many years in a parish where I never heard an oath ... Nobody complained more of our church government than our taverners, whose ordinary lamentation was, their trade was broke, people were become so sober.
>
> (Fyfe, 1928, pp. 242–3)

The Act Recissory abolished all laws passed since 1633, removing both Covenanting reforms and the most obnoxious of Charles I's legislation. Charles II turned to aristocrats and landlords to govern Scotland. It was thus necessary for him to rely on a group of men many of whom had been committed opponents of his father as moderate Covenanters. This was a notable contrast with England, where those aristocrats who gathered round the court had Anglican and royalist credentials.

Ireland

The Irish convention was summoned in Dublin by a group of English officers. It was these people who were to be best rewarded by the terms of the Restoration, disappointing the hopes of members of the Catholic Confederation of Kilkenny who thought that, because they had protested their faithfulness to the monarchy and stood by the young Charles II, the king would recognise their loyalty in tangible form. It was a combination of land and religion that dominated the Restoration settlement in Ireland, but land proved much the most intractable subject.

The Church of Ireland was restored and Catholic hopes of toleration were quickly dashed, though, as in England, the extent of persecution fluctuated. A pressing problem was that of nonconformity (primarily Scots Presbyterians in Ulster). During the 1650s, there had been a tendency to assume that any Protestant minister was preferable to a Catholic, so a very wide range of people had served the Protestant ministry. From 1666, all clergy had to conform to an Act of Uniformity requiring the use of the Book of Common Prayer and episcopal ordination for clergy. The Presbyterians in Ulster greeted the return of Church of Ireland bishops with dismay, and a good many clergy were ejected. They were also affected by the religious turmoil in Scotland.

The Catholics' chief concern was not the religious settlement, from which they knew they could expect nothing once it became apparent that there was no chance of toleration, but the land settlement. In Ireland, the criteria for judging how to allocate land after the Restoration were utterly different from those used in England. Much Irish land had been confiscated from Catholic rebels and granted to English settlers. Some of this had been in the form of direct grants, some had been in the form of debentures issued to English parliamentary soldiers in lieu of pay. In fact, few soldiers took their allocations of land; instead, they sold their debentures chiefly to people who already had some interest in Ireland. So, while there had been a considerable redistribution of land from Catholics and Protestant royalists to Protestant supporters of parliament, the population of Protestants was not greatly enlarged but those who were already there became richer and more influential. The principle of the Restoration land settlement was simple. It was to prefer Protestant landowners to Catholic, so lands were restored to Protestant royalists and a few 'innocent papists'. But the terms were difficult to implement, and several additional Acts had to be passed to effect them, because allowing Protestants to retain their land and meeting the claims of royalists and worthy Catholics proved impossible with the amount of land available.

EXERCISE

From which quarters of society in the British Isles might Charles have expected opposition?

Spend about 10 minutes on this exercise.

SPECIMEN ANSWER

In England, from royalists disappointed by the lack of restitution of their property, and from Protestant nonconformists; in Scotland, from former Covenanters; in Ireland, from Catholics who regarded themselves as loyal to the monarchy and from Presbyterians.

As we shall see, few of these groups, with the exception of the Covenanters in Scotland, were to cause much difficulty. Rather, opposition came from people who might reasonably have been supposed to be Charles's supporters.

OPPOSITION

Charles II: England

Charles had a good political nose for survival and had no intention of being sent on his travels again. For much of his reign he put up with the opposition of nonconformists who were not, in the main, politically dangerous: most of them simply aspired to freedom of worship and to being recognised as citizens. In any case, they amounted to no more than about 5 per cent of the population. Only Quakers had been singled out for particular attention under the terms of the Clarendon Code. A rising of the radical sect called the Fifth Monarchy Men in 1661, and the Farnley Wood Plot of 1663 by a group of Presbyterians, gave the government no real cause for concern, but the administration was extremely responsive to rumour, and news of the activities of regicides in exile on the continent was sufficient to cause ripples in England.

The greatest subject for rumour was Catholic activity. It was Catholics who were, both directly and indirectly, to cause Charles most difficulty. Sympathetic to them – it was rumoured that even if he was not a secret Catholic during his lifetime, he made a deathbed conversion – he wanted on grounds of both tolerance and expediency to alleviate their position. But English prejudices flourished about the absolutist ambitions of the king of France, Louis XIV (*1643–1715), at whose court the young Charles had spent a period of his exile, and the potential for this formative example, along with blood ties (the two kings were cousins), to maintain a hold on Charles II. These fears were fed by tales of a Jesuit plot behind the Great Fire of London (1666), and there is no doubt that anti-Catholicism provided a suitable banner behind which Protestants of all shades of opinion could unite to heal the rifts of the 1640s and 1650s. In point of fact, there can have been little real risk since Catholics formed no more than 2 per cent of the population.

Three episodes raised particular anti-Catholic fury. The first was in 1672, when Charles, as a result of secret negotiations for a financial subsidy from Louis XIV, issued a Declaration of Indulgence, suspending the operation of the laws against Catholics and, incidentally, against nonconformists. Both judges and Commons objected to the legality of the measure. Charles had to withdraw the Indulgence and agree to the Test Act, which required all office holders not only to swear allegiance to the king and recognise that he was head of the church but also to provide documentary proof that they had taken the Anglican sacraments. The Test Act led to the second episode, when it was revealed, in 1673, that James, duke of York, Charles's brother and heir to the throne, had converted to Catholicism. This had no immediate consequences, not least because James's heirs were his two Protestant daughters, but the prospect of a Catholic ruler was destabilising. The third episode was an outstanding example of the power of rumour: the Popish Plot. In 1678, plans for a supposed Jesuit plot to assassinate the king were revealed to the government. Neither the revealers of the plot nor anyone else associated with it had any credibility, nor was there any foundation to the revelation. But such was the power of anti-Catholic feeling that for some months fears gripped the population, including parliament. These fears gave grounds for a proposal to exclude James, duke of York, from the succession to the throne and install as heir in his place, James, duke of Monmouth, Charles's illegitimate son. Charles was implacably opposed to setting aside the succession, not least because to allow inheritance by an illegitimate child would be to cause major difficulties for many propertied families. Bills were introduced in parliament in 1680 and 1681. The first was defeated in the House of Lords and the second was lost when Charles dissolved parliament.

What also aroused anxiety was not solely a religious matter, but also a constitutional one. Charles had first attempted to issue a Declaration of Indulgence in 1662, realising that religious toleration measures were unlikely to be get through parliament. He withdrew after taking legal advice from the judiciary, who doubted the legality of such a move. They had not changed their mind when he tried again in 1672; this time both judges and parliament expressed their view that laws could only be suspended by statute. No one doubted that he had the power to dispense a few individuals from the operation of such a law, but suspending statute law tested the extent of the king's powers in parliament. Although the suspending power was contested, the king's unchallenged power to dissolve parliament gave him considerable control. Whether Charles's use of these devices shows tendencies towards absolutism is questionable.

We saw in Unit 10 how ecclesiastical visitations were used to keep track of the religion and morality of the population. Such visitations continued to be conducted in the Restoration church, but rather more intermittently. Charles II's lord treasurer, beset by anxieties about the strength of the Church of England under the new regime, seems to have been behind the decision of the archbishop of Canterbury, Gilbert Sheldon, to commission an ecclesiastical survey, 'the counting of noses', in 1675. Lord Treasurer Danby evidently wanted to persuade the king of the need to continue to support the Church of England by demonstrating through statistics that it had the support of the majority of the population. The Compton Census, as it is called (after Henry Compton, bishop of London), was sent round to all parishes in England, who were asked to record the number of people in each parish, the number of popish recusants (Catholics) and the number of Protestant nonconformists.

This national survey is of great importance because, apart from the figures for each religious group, it allows estimates of the population to be made for an era before censuses. However, it is not a simple source to use: in some parishes, the clergyman or church warden counted families or households rather than individuals; there was no clear guidance about the age at which people should be included (usually anyone over the age of 16); many dissenters may not have been included because they sometimes attended Anglican services. However, this is not a reason for not using the source, but a reason for trying to understand it better.

Online exercise

To see how historians can use material such as this, you should now go to the A200 website to examine spreadsheets containing statistics from the Compton Census. You will find tutorials taking you through the statistics together with instructions on how to get started on the website.

This work together with the exercise below is likely to take you about 4 hours.

EXERCISE

Now that you have worked through the figures for the Compton Census and seen the proportions of Catholics and nonconformists, consider why the activities of Catholics and nonconformists were so conspicuous.

SPECIMEN ANSWER

England was still a confessional state with an established church. The members of its government and parliament after the Test Act had to be practising members of that church. So it was still possible to equate Protestant or Catholic dissent from the Church of England with disloyalty, even though Charles II made no claims to divine right.

DISCUSSION

All the laws about church attendance that had been in force in Charles I's reign remained on the statute book and were reinforced by the legislation of the Clarendon Code. The church courts, which had been responsible for prosecutions for non-attendance at church, had not regained their prewar effectiveness and most prosecutions were under the Clarendon Code laws. But one prewar anxiety that had not gone away was that of continental Catholicism and its associations with absolutism. Louis XIV's actions were watched with interest and his control of the government of France and his territorial ambitions were viewed with suspicion.

Charles II: Scotland and Ireland

In Scotland, the most pressing problem remained the religious settlement, which had been imposed from above. Covenanters who refused to accept the reinstatement of bishops were forbidden to meet outside the official services of the Church of Scotland by the Act against conventicles (illegal religious assemblies), while former ministers were prevented from living within 20 miles of their former flocks. In the south-west, where conventicles were particularly common, military force was used to break up meetings and enforce the payment of fines. The Pentland Rising and the defeat of Covenanters in 1666 at Rullion Green led to a more conciliatory policy (though many rebels were shipped to Barbados). However, during the period 1674–79, repression was renewed with a law that required landlords and masters to take responsibility for the religious conformity of their tenants and employees.

Widespread opposition in the south-west led to the imposition of the Highland Host in 1678, under which soldiers were quartered on recalcitrant communities. In 1679, the Covenanters assassinated the archbishop of St Andrews and rose in armed rebellion; they were defeated at Bothwell Brig (22 June 1679) by the king's forces under the command of his illegitimate son, the duke of Monmouth. Further repression took place in the early 1680s, partly in response to the emergence of a radical group known as Cameronians, who disowned the king and engaged in guerrilla warfare. Like the Catholic fury in England, the Covenanting fury in Scotland made more noise than action, but nevertheless was deeply divisive.

The 1681 Test Act required anyone elected or appointed to office to acknowledge the royal supremacy of the Church of Scotland. But no attempt was made in Scotland to set aside the succession of James, duke of York, for that of James, duke of Monmouth. Had any of the English Exclusion Bills passed, it would have had no legal jurisdiction in Scotland, and the duke of York would have remained heir to the Scottish throne.

In Ireland, initially the Church of Ireland commanded all official support, but in the course of the 1660s there was substantial toleration of Catholics provided they demonstrated that they were loyal to the king, as many of the Irish aristocracy did. Irish Catholic churchmen were caught up in the anti-Catholic fury generated by the Popish Plot, but the Presbyterians lived peaceably.

James II and VII

> **James II and VII** (*1685–1701) was Charles II's younger brother. In 1660, he married Anne Hyde, daughter of Charles II's minister the earl of Clarendon. The couple had two daughters, Mary, who married her cousin Prince William of Orange, and Anne, who married George, a Danish prince. Anne Hyde died in 1671 and, having converted to Catholicism in 1673, James married the Catholic Princess Mary of Modena, who gave birth to a son in 1688. Between 1679 and 1682 he lived in Scotland. Following his flight in 1688, he lived in exile in France.

Unease at James II and VII's accession in 1685, illustrated by Monmouth's rising in the south-west of England, is a telling reminder that the question of religion and, most particularly, whether the peoples of a state could feel secure in their chosen confession if it was not shared by their ruler, had not been settled either by the Civil Wars or the 1660 Restoration settlement. During his brief reign, James managed to turn many of the most loyal supporters of the Anglican church and the Stuart monarchy into his opponents. The sorry arrival in England of French Protestant refugees (the Huguenots) after Louis XIV had revoked, in October 1685, France's equivalent of the Toleration Act, the Edict of Nantes,[1] brought renewed horror stories of the sufferings of Protestants at the hands of Catholics. As with the pamphlets of the Thirty Years War and depositions of the 1641 Irish Uprising (Unit 10, pp. 27, 58), these raised the spectre of Catholic absolutism as a distinct threat. James managed to confirm these fears and reminded everyone of the constitutional infractions of his father, Charles I. He had come to the throne in a very strong position in England, for his brother's reform of municipal corporations, to influence parliamentary elections, ensured that members of James's first parliament were unprecedentedly compliant; yet within three years he provoked a revolution. How did this happen?

James appointed Catholic officers to the army raised against Monmouth; he secured a judgement allowing him to dispense individuals from the Test Act; he suspended the English penal laws against Catholics and nonconformists with Declarations of Indulgence in 1687 and 1688; he attempted to get Magdalen College, Oxford, to accept a Catholic president. These measures roused, one by one, the ecclesiastical, judicial and parliamentary establishment. Seven Anglican bishops, who had petitioned against the order to read the Declaration of Indulgence from the pulpit, were prosecuted for seditious libel; senior judges who repeatedly found against his right to suspend laws were dismissed; and the fellows of Magdalen College were deprived of their fellowships.

Archibald Campbell, 9th earl of Argyll (executed 1685) was a great territorial magnate in the Highlands and associated with the radical Covenanters. He was prosecuted for various crimes which had primarily to do with his political influence in the Highlands. Having escaped, he led a rising against James II and VII in 1685 and was executed.

James had effectively been ruling Scotland from 1681, appointed as lord high commissioner by his brother, but at his accession a Highland rising led by the earl of Argyll, and loosely connected with Monmouth's rising, broke out. James's first parliament took a strong line against the rebellious Covenanters and declared attendance at conventicles punishable by death. He introduced Catholics into a number of important positions in the country and announced

---

[1] The Edict of Nantes, issued on 13 April 1598 by the French king Henry IV was aimed at ending the French Wars of Religion by granting limited toleration to Protestants (Huguenots). They were guaranteed protection under the law at home, protection from the Inquisition abroad and full *civil* rights (including the right to state employment). However, Catholicism was affirmed as the official state religion and freedom of Protestant worship limited to certain geographical areas of France.

that as parliament would not cooperate in giving Catholics freedom of worship, he would use his prerogative. His first measure for religious toleration in Scotland was confined to Catholics and Quakers, but the Declaration of Indulgence (1687) extended freedom of worship in private houses to non-Church-of-Scotland Presbyterians (i.e. Covenanters). James was strongly opposed in the Privy Council and by the Church of Scotland – two bishops were sacked for their opposition and anti-Catholic violence broke out in Edinburgh.

James's accession was 'received with joy by Irish Catholics, and with corresponding gloom by Protestants' (Simms, 1978b, p. 478). However, he did not attempt to overturn the Protestant land settlement of his predecessors, seeing it as a guarantee of continued English, and thus royal, power in Ireland. He did, though, grant a number of commissions to Catholics in the Irish army and advanced the fortunes of the Catholic Richard Talbot, earl of Tyrconnell. Tyrconnell purged the army of Protestant rank and file and replaced them with Catholics. By 1687, the majority of judges and privy councillors in Ireland were Catholics. Catholics were installed as county sheriffs, responsible for parliamentary elections, ensuring that the next Irish House of Commons would be predominantly Catholic.

These measures were distasteful to Irish Protestants – both Anglicans and Presbyterians – as they excluded them from positions of power, influence and profit, but they were not actively damaging. James's policy of leaving Church of Ireland vacancies unfilled and using the income to subsidise Catholic clergy roused complaints. But what created a party of opposition to James was the rumour that the land settlement was to be altered to give Catholics sufficient land to secure them in the face of a possible Protestant succession on James's death. The rumour was given substance in 1688, when it was proposed that half of the Cromwellian land grants should be revoked in favour of Catholics, but that it was not at that moment expedient to hold a parliament in Ireland to enact this reform.

Revolt

It was the English whose dissatisfaction with James II was so great that it stimulated a group of English notables to think the unthinkable and open negotiations with Prince William of Orange, husband of James II's elder daughter Mary (see Figure 12.2). Or was it unthinkable? Once one king had been despatched, doing it again seemed a distinct (though undesirable) possibility. The critical event was the birth of a son to King James and his queen in 1688 – a son who would be brought up as a Catholic, removing the prospect of a return to Protestant monarchy at James's death. Then, in October 1688, James ordered four regiments from Ireland to England. Not only were the troops disorderly but they raised ghosts of Charles I's use of Irish forces and of the unrestrained use of the royal prerogative. By themselves, these events might not have precipitated the invitation to William; it was the record

Figure 12.2   Wax likenesses of William III and Mary II from Westminster Abbey, his modelled from life, hers from her death mask. Photo: © Dean and Chapter of Westminster

of James's intransigence and insensitivity to his subjects' worries that made this the occasion.

It is arguable that many of the political and religious difficulties experienced by Charles II and James II arose from unfinished business at the Restoration. But William's keenness to secure England as an ally in his European venture against France made him an enthusiast for approaches from England. He had been in touch with a number of leading English politicians for some years before seven leading politicians wrote to him to propose that he would be supported if he led an expedition to England to secure a free parliament. There are parallels with the return of Charles II in 1660, of succession led by invitation of parliamentarians, but responses within the three kingdoms and the settlements reached had some noticeable differences.

> **William of Orange** (1650–1702) succeeded his father, William II, as prince of Orange and ruler in the Netherlands, and was leader of the coalition of European states opposing Louis XIV's plans to extend France's territorial borders. He was a nephew of Charles II and James II, and married James's eldest daughter, Mary. In 1688, by invitation, he arrived in England and was declared monarch jointly with his wife. He subdued Scotland and Ireland. He used his position as king to continue to pursue military campaigns against Louis XIV of France. After Mary's death in 1694, he was declared king in his own right.

FOR WHOM WAS THE GLORIOUS REVOLUTION EITHER GLORIOUS OR A REVOLUTION?

William of Orange's arrival at Torbay was not greeted with the elation shown on Charles II's return. John Evelyn recorded on 5 November 1688 'These are the beginnings of great sorrow, unless God in his mercy prevent it by some happy reconciliation of all dissentions amongst us' (Evelyn, n.d., pp. 660). But for many English people, his arrival was a relief from the threat of popery and arbitrary rule.

England

William's arrival in England led to a speedy settlement; a convention declared the throne vacant, offered William and Mary the throne, and drew up the Declaration of Rights, later passed as the Bill of Rights. Most of the required legislation was passed during the year following: confirming the ascendancy of Protestantism; requiring that holders of any elected positions and government offices take Anglican communion; and offering toleration (through the Toleration Act) without civil rights to Protestant dissenters. The Mutiny Act declared that a standing army might only be kept in peacetime with the consent of parliament. By the time that William's first parliament met in 1691, constitutional matters had been settled on a pragmatic basis and without bloodshed. But it could not be said that William's rule was secure in either Scotland or Ireland.

One transformation that William's reign achieved was that both monarch and people were united in regarding Louis XIV's France as the enemy. For William, one of the most appealing aspects of the English crown was that he could bring England into the continental anti-French alliance. Both Charles II and James II had wanted to conduct a pro-French foreign policy, which was much opposed by parliament, and both kings received substantial financial subsidies from Louis as the price of staying out of Europe. It would be difficult to claim by this time that there was any real sense of a Protestant alliance, though it happened that a good many of the states lined up against France happened to be Protestant.

Scotland

At the news that James II had fled, crowds in Edinburgh broke down the Catholic furnishings at the royal chapel in Holyrood House, but the assumption of power by William and Mary in Scotland was a much less clearly defined event than it was in England. One historian of the period avers that 'The Revolution was made in England and imported to Scotland' (Donaldson, 1978 [1965], p. 383) – an English decision to which Scots were invited to react.

A Convention of Estates was called in March 1689, and initially neither Jacobites nor Williamites commanded a majority. William assured the convention of his desire to secure Protestantism, while James issued threats to those who forsook allegiance to him, thus turning many waverers towards William. William and Mary were declared monarchs in Scotland in April and accepted the Claim of Right, though its status as a constitutional document was open to question. The different priorities of Scotland and England can be summed up in the differences between the Scottish Claim of Right and the English Bill of Rights. Both documents were drawn up by assemblies of peers and commons and have many similarities, and there are identical passages in them. But the differences between the concerns of the two countries become apparent when we look at the list of complaints against King James (see Table 12.2).

Table 12.2   Complaints made against James II and VII in the Bill of Rights and the Claim of Right

	English Bill of Rights	Scottish Claim of Right
1	By assuming and exercising a power of dispensing with and suspending of laws, and the execution of laws, without consent of parliament	By erecting public schools, and societies of Jesuits; and not only allowing mass to be publicly said, but also inverting [converting] Protestant chapels and churches to public mass houses, contrary to the express laws against saying and hearing of mass

2	By committing and prosecuting divers worthy prelates, for humbly petitioning to be excused concurring to the said assumed power	By allowing popish books to be printed, and dispersed, by a gift to a popish printer; designing him printer to his Majesty's household, college and chapel, contrary to the law
3	By issuing and causing to be executed a commission under the great seal for erecting a court called, The court of commissioners for ecclesiastical causes	By taking children of Protestant noblemen and gentlemen, sending and keeping them abroad, to be bred papists ... bestowing pensions upon priests, and perverting Protestants from their religion, by offers of places, preferments and pensions
4	By levying money for and to the use of the crown, by pretence of prerogative, for other time, and in other manner, than the same was granted by parliament	By disarming Protestants, while at the same time he employed papists, in the places of greatest trust, civil and military, such as Chancellor, Secretaries, Privy Councillors, and Lords of Session, thrusting out Protestants, to make room for papists, and entrusting the forts and magazines of the kingdom in their hands
5	By raising and keeping a standing army within this kingdom on time of peace, without consent of parliament, and quartering soldiers contrary to law	By imposing oaths contrary to law
6	By causing several good subjects, being Protestant, to be disarmed, at the same time when papists were both armed and employed, contrary to law	By giving gifts and grants for exacting money, without consent of parliament, or Convention of Estates
7	By violating the freedom of election of members to serve in parliament	By levying, or keeping on foot, a standing army in time of peace, without consent of parliament, which army did exact locality, free and dry quarters
8	By prosecutions in the court of King's Bench, for matters and causes cognizable only in parliament; and by divers other arbitrary and illegal courses	By employing the officers of the army, as judges through the kingdom, and by imposing them where there were heritable [feudal] offices and jurisdictions, by whom many of the lieges were put to death summarily, without legal trial, jury or record
9	And whereas of late years, partial, corrupt, and unqualified persons have been returned and served on juries in trials and particularly divers jurors in trials for high treason, which were not freeholders	By imposing exorbitant fines, to the values of parties' estates, exacting extravagant bail, and disposing fines and forfaultures [forfeitures] before any process or conviction
10	And excessive bail hath been required of persons committed in criminal cases, to elude the benefit of the laws made for the liberty of the subjects	By imprisoning persons without expressing the reason, and delaying to put them on trial
11	And excessive fines have been imposed; and illegal and cruel punishments inflicted	By causing pursue and forfault [forfeit] several persons upon stretches of old and obsolete laws, upon frivolous and weak pretences, upon lame and defective probations, as particularly the earl of Argyll, to the scandal and reproach of the justice of the nation

12 And several grants and promises made of fines and forfeitures, before any conviction or judgement against the persons, upon whom the same were to be levied	By subverting the right of the royal burghs, the third estate of parliament, imposing upon them not only magistrates, but also the whole town council, and clerks, contrary to their liberties ... so that the commissioners to parliament, being chosen by the magistrates and council, the king might well in effect nominate that entire estate of parliament; and many of the said magistrates put in by him, were avowed papists
	By sending letters to the chief court of justice, not only ordaining the judges to stop and desist *sine die* [until further notice] to determine causes, but also ordering and commanding them how to proceed, in cases depending before them, contrary to the express laws, and by changing the nature of the judges gifts *ad vitam aut culpam* [for life or for cause], and giving them commissions *ad bene placitum* [at pleasure], to dispose them to compliance and arbitrary courses, and turning them out of their offices when they did not comply
	By granting personal protection for civil debts contrary to law

All of which are utterly and directly contrary to the known laws, statutes and freedoms of this realm

(Sources: Williams, 1960, pp. 26–27; *The Declaration of the Estates of the Kingdom of Scotland Containing the Claim of Right, and the Offer of the Crown to Their Majesties, King William and Queen Mary*, 1689, Edinburgh, pp. 3–4)

EXERCISE

Look at the list of complaints made against the king in Table 12.2 (we have retained the order of the original documents so you may find that the same complaints appear in both documents but in different places). What can we learn about the different priorities of the two nations?

Spend about 20 minutes on this exercise.

SPECIMEN ANSWER

The Scottish document gives greatest emphasis to James's crimes against Protestantism, while the English document focuses much more on his violation of the law and infringement of parliament's powers.

DISCUSSION

It is possible that the Scottish parliament gave rise to less passion because it was less powerful than the parliament of England. It would appear from the emphasis in the Scottish list given to the law courts and judges that they were a more important guarantee of subjects' freedoms than parliament. What we don't learn from this list is what constitutional terms were actually agreed on.

Support for King James came from Scottish bishops, who realised that without him their future was doomed. But the Scottish episcopate had come to represent arbitrary royal rule in a way quite unlike their English counterparts. James also had the support of his loyal servant Viscount Dundee and his Highland army. Dundee was killed at the battle of Killiecrankie (1689), though his force was victorious there. His troops staggered on for a bit, without much verve, but the presence of such military opposition made it necessary for William to keep the Scottish parliament loyal to vote money to allow a royal army to be maintained in Scotland. The final act in the suppression of the rebellious Highlanders, a spectacular propaganda failure, was the massacre of Glencoe in which thirty-eight Highlanders were killed by William's military forces, whom they had accommodated for the past fortnight.

Ireland

There was no neat exchange of kings in Ireland either, where James II's reign lingered on for another three years with a bitter war, aspects of which colour political and community relations in Northern Ireland to this day.

James's flight to France and Louis XIV's offer of help with an invasion of Ireland immediately made the conquest of Ireland an imperative in William's European policy. James landed in Ireland in March 1689; the English navy failed to prevent this and a later force from landing.

Derry, having become the main centre of Protestant resistance, needed to be subdued, and in April the siege began, effectively a blockade by Catholic troops of a walled city sheltering some 20,000 soldiers and civilians. Three regiments of Protestant troops failed to dislodge the besieging Catholics; finally, on 28 July, the Protestant forces approached the city up the river, and after 105 days the city was relieved.

This episode was rapidly presented as a tale of heroic resistance, The acting governor, a Church of Ireland clergyman, George Walker, travelled to London and was presented to the king after a triumphant progress through Scotland and northern England. While in London, he published an account of the siege that appeared in at least three English editions in 1689, as well as in Scottish, Dutch and German editions. He published other works of Protestant polemic as well (see Figure 12.3).

EXERCISE

Read Anthology Document 3.21, 'Extract from George Walker's account of the siege of Derry, 1689'.

1   What effect would such publications as these have (note particularly the dates and places of publication)?

2   How were these effects achieved?

Spend about 30 minutes on this exercise.

SPECIMEN ANSWER

1   Walker was particularly prized as a propagandist in the war against Catholicism: for those who were doubtful about rebelling against the hereditary king, Walker's account assured them of the horrors of the Catholics. The account was rushed out within a few weeks and was published in those places where it might strengthen the Protestant cause. Defeating James was part of the European war against Louis XIV in which William was engaged, hence the publication of editions on the continent where it might be read by anti-French allies.

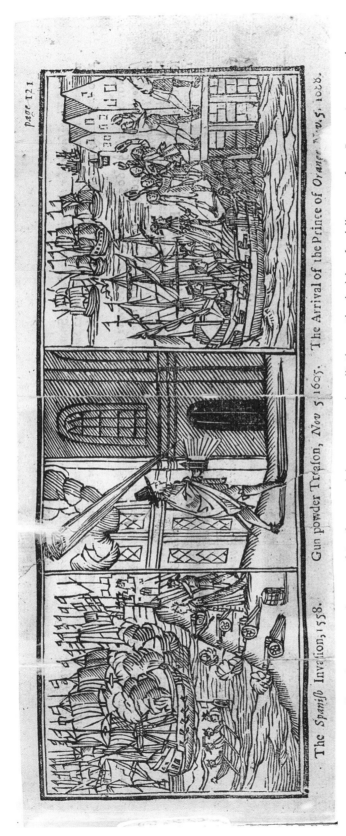

Figure 12.3   George Walker, *The Protestant's Crums of Comfort, containing prayers and meditations … thanksgivings for deliverances from Popery, tyranny and arbitrary power … illustrated with pictures suitable to each particular occasion*, London, 1690, picture facing p.121 featuring 'The Spanish Invasion, 1558'; 'Gun powder Treason, Nov 5 1605'; 'The Arrival of the Prince of Orange, Nov. 5 1688'. Photo: The British Library. The illustrations connect the siege explicitly with earlier episodes when a Roman Catholic threat was defeated. George Walker was governor of Londonderry (as it was called at the time) during the siege

2   Walker used the form of a diary (we don't know if he had actually kept one in this form). It is the diary details – the gradual diminution in the number of men, the list of unpalatable food with its prices – that provide such a vivid account of the hardships of the besieged population. The account consciously draws on a tradition of anti-Catholic propaganda of a type we saw in Unit 10 in connection with the 1641 rising. He attributes the victory to God and cowardice to the enemy who ran away in the night.

DISCUSSION

Walker's account was not published in Ireland, and proved to be controversial. A Presbyterian minister, John Mackenzie, who was chaplain to one of the regiments in Derry, published a critique of Walker for taking too much credit for himself and giving not enough to the Presbyterians. Another pamphlet attempted to give credit to Colonel Michelburne as joint commander with Walker, saying of Walker that his 'conduct appeared more conspicuous in the eating part than the fighting, and reason good, the charge of the stores, and provision being committed to him alone' (*An Account*, 1692, 'Epistle to the reader', unpaginated).

Despite the Protestant victory at Derry and success at Enniskillen, the Irish Jacobites held out, so William sent the duke of Schomberg in August 1689 with a force. The two sides were evenly matched, so William arrived himself in June 1690, having sent over a further 7,000 soldiers in advance. James's forces, with French reinforcements, would have matched these had not Louis XIV required that the same number of Irish troops be sent to France. On 1 July, the two armies met in the Boyne Valley, north of Dublin. Anthology Document 3.22, 'A Jacobite account of the battle of the Boyne, 1690', is an account of the Jacobite defeat written by an Englishman serving in James's army.

James fled to France on 4 July and William took control of Dublin and eastern Ireland. The siege of Limerick, bravely held by the Catholic forces within, reinvigorated the Jacobites, as did William's return to England, but at the same time the French army left. The war continued into the next year with a crushing defeat of the Jacobites at Aughrim (30 June 1691) and a second siege of Limerick. The Treaty of Limerick (3 October 1691) marked the final surrender of James's armies.

The most striking effects of the Williamite victory were in the intensification of religious divisions and in the land settlement, which continued the work of the early seventeenth-century and Cromwellian transfers of land from Catholics to Protestants. The Treaty of Limerick offered Catholics freedom of worship consistent with the laws of Ireland, or as they had enjoyed in Charles II's reign, and assured the property of Jacobites who took an oath of allegiance to William and remained in Ireland. The penal laws that were eventually enacted were regarded as a breach of faith in that persecution of Catholics intensified. At the same time, Protestants who were not members of the Church of Ireland (chiefly Ulster Presbyterians who were nearly as numerous as Anglicans and whose numbers were growing through emigration from Scotland), were not granted anything comparable to the English Toleration Act. Dissenters were, however, able to vote and sit in the Irish parliament but not in local municipal corporations; but, for the most part, Presbyterians were too poor to be involved in parliament.

James II had allowed Irish Catholics to think that there might be some renegotiation of earlier land settlements. Subsequently, William made some very large grants of land in Ireland to his foreign associates. These were cancelled by the English parliament, an action that caused much annoyance in Ireland, especially to the people who had bought land from the recipients of William's generosity. The Williamite transfer of land was not as extensive as that agreed under the Restoration settlement, but the largest transfers took place in the richest provinces of Leinster and Munster. The effects were compounded by legislation that prevented Catholics from purchasing land or leasing it for more than 31 years. Any land owned by Catholics could only be passed on by inheritance if it was divided equally between all possible male heirs. This had the effect of reducing the size of individual Catholics' property holdings. The effects of this can be seen in Table 12.3.

Table 12.3   Percentage of land owned by Catholics in Ireland

1641	60%
1675	22%
1703	14%

(Sources: Simms, 1978a, p. 426; Simms, 1986, p. 12)

The settlement in Ireland was not achieved simply by the Treaty of Limerick but by a sequence of legislation over the succeeding twenty years which assured that: Protestants who had acquired land confiscated from Catholics had secure tenure; members of the Church of Ireland had a monopoly of civil and military offices; only Protestants could sit in the Irish parliament. The Irish House of Commons tried to extend its power as a result of meeting more often to vote taxation for the king, but it did so in the interests only of a very narrow range of people who remained in control of the country for the best part of a century.

CONCLUSION

The Commonwealth had revolutionary objectives, even if it did not (in the end) manage to cement a new form of state. The drawing up of a first written constitution, the Instrument of Government, and an amalgamated parliament of representatives from England, Wales, Scotland and Ireland indicate the ambitions of the Protectorate to create a new, unitary state in the British Isles, even if neither long survived the death of Oliver Cromwell. And constitutional experiments continued after 1660; it is important to stress that Charles II's return to the throne may have reinstated the monarchy, but was not a total return to the *status quo ante bellum* (situation before the war). Despite the king's resolute pursuit of the regicides, those who had signed his father's death warrant, and thirst for revenge so strong that it extended to exhuming the bodies of dead regicides (including Cromwell) for mock executions, the impact of the Commonwealth years on the political framework of the three kingdoms was not completely wiped out by the Restoration.

The restoration in 1660 of the monarchy, the three-kingdom federated state and the established Protestant church impacted differently on England, Scotland and Ireland, as did the constitutional difficulties posed by the succession in 1685 of a Catholic head of state in James II and VII. That being so, we will conclude this unit by summarising the condition of the state within the three kingdoms in this period, and considering what changes took place between the Restoration and the reign of William and Mary, and to what causes we might attribute these changes.

EXERCISE

Look now at Table 12.4 below and, thinking about the comparable tables for the earlier periods (Table 9.1 and Table 12.1), answer the following questions:

1   Were there any changes in the claims of any of the nations to be states?

2   What changes had taken place by 1691?

Spend about 30 minutes on this exercise.

Table 12.4   Changes in England (with Wales), Scotland and Ireland between the reigns of Charles I and William and Mary

	England and Wales	**Scotland**	**Ireland**
Ruler			
Restoration settlement and Charles II	Charles II, *1660–85 (his reign was officially dated from the death of Charles I in 1649). Hereditary succession challenged by attempts from 1679 to make Charles's illegitimate son the duke of Monmouth heir in place of his brother James, duke of York.	Charles II declared king in Scotland in 1649 and crowned there 1651, but did not rule until 1660. From 1681, James, duke of York, was king's commissioner in Scotland.	Charles II declared king in 1649 but did not rule until 1660. Royal authority was represented by lord lieutenant/lord deputy.
James II and VII	James II, *1685–88. James fled, on the strength of which the hereditary succession was set aside to prevent his Catholic son succeeding him.	Reigned as James VII.	Lord lieutenant/lord deputy Catholic earl of Tyrconnell, 1687–90. James II fled to Ireland in 1689 and remained there until defeated by William III at the Boyne, 1690.

William III and Mary and the Revolution settlement	No amendment of constitution required to admit William III and Mary, *1688–1702. Mary had a claim to the throne as daughter of James II, but her husband continued to rule after her death in 1694. After 1689, ideas of contract rather than divine right prevailed. Protestant succession was assured under 1701 Act of Settlement following death of James II in exile and of the son of Anne (nearest Protestant male heir).	Reigned as William II.	Lord lieutenant/lord deputy Sidney, 1690–95.

Legislature

Restoration settlement and Charles II	Parliament meeting at Westminster consisting of House of Lords (peers and bishops) and House of Commons (1 member for each borough and 2 for each county elected by men owning freeholds worth more than 40 shillings/£2). Right to call and dismiss parliament was monarch's alone but limited by 1664 Triennial Act. Charles flouted Act after 1684.	Single chamber parliament meeting in Edinburgh consisting of Scottish peers (whose numbers doubled 1603–1707), 14 bishops and burgesses representing burghs (royal burghs increased from 50 to 67). Right to call and dismiss parliament was king's, proceedings dominated by Lords of the Articles (restored 1661). Rival assemblies (such as the Convention of Royal Burghs and the General Assembly of the Kirk) were also able to legislate. 1661 Act Recissory rescinded all legislation since 1633. Parliament began to operate more as a debating chamber and less as a place to approve reports of Committee of Articles.	Parliament meeting in Dublin consisting of House of Lords (peers and bishops) and House of Commons. From 1661, Commons exclusively Protestant. Right to call and dismiss parliament was lord lieutenant's.

Legislature (cont'd)

James II and VII	Inherited compliant parliament because of changes made in Charles II's last years.	In 1686, James asked parliament to set aside civil disabilities for Catholics.	James II, after fleeing England, called a Catholic parliament in Dublin, which sat May–July 1689 and declared all English legislation to be inapplicable to Ireland but did not repeal Poyning's Law.
William III and Mary and the Revolution settlement	Convention met. Triennial Act 1694 required meetings of parliament every 3 years. After 1707, members for Scottish constituencies sat in Commons and a selected number of Scottish peers in the Lords.	Convention of Estates met in 1689. Committee of Articles abolished in 1689, reducing crown's ability to manage parliament. Bishops excluded in 1689. Scottish parliament abolished in 1707.	William's parliaments met more frequently and voted supply more often. Membership restricted to Protestants from 1691, but Catholics could vote in elections. By 1725, 9 of 127 lay peers were Catholic.

Judiciary

Restoration settlement and Charles II	Judges appointed at king's pleasure. Church courts restored but used much less. Habeas Corpus Amendment Act 1679.	Judges appointed at king's pleasure. Patchwork of ancient local courts, many dependent on landlords.	Judges appointed at king's pleasure.
James II and VII	Dismissed judges at pleasure. Appointed Catholics to the bench.		Appointed 3 Catholic judges.
William III and Mary and the Revolution settlement	1691, opposition to royal control of judiciary.		

Executive

Restoration settlement and Charles II	Privy Council and ministers chosen by king.	During process of restoration, executive directed by committee of English Privy Council. After 1660, king controlled all appointments to executive (posts mainly held by aristocrats).	Committee of English Privy Council for Irish Affairs directed administration.
James II and VII	Privy Council and ministers chosen by king.	Catholics appointed to influential offices.	Catholics admitted to municipal corporations and appointed sheriffs.
William III and Mary and the Revolution settlement	Privy Council and ministers chosen by king.	King controlled appointments.	King controlled appointments.

Foreign policy

Restoration settlement and Charles II	Directed by king in London.	Directed by king in London.	Directed by king in London.
James II and VII	Directed by king in London.	Directed by king in London.	Directed by king in London.
William III and Mary and the Revolution settlement	William's foreign policy dominated by maintaining anti-French coalition of European states.	Foreign policy directed from London.	Foreign policy directed from London aimed at preventing Irish Jacobite–French alliance.

Defence

Restoration settlement and Charles II	Return to decentralised militia administered in counties. Militia Act 1662 gave crown control of armed forces.	Last English troops left in 1662. Small army retained; after 1667, militia controlled by nobility. Private fiefdoms of Highland nobles left alone. King had power to make war and peace and to make all military appointments.	Protestant force kept in arms, latterly Protestant dissenters excluded. Catholics served in English forces abroad. Protestant militia for home defence.
James II and VII	James demanded that Catholics be given commissions in the army.	Command of Edinburgh Castle given to a Catholic.	James gave commissions to Catholic officers; eventually 2/3 of army was Catholic. Catholic earl of Tyrconnell made lieutenant general of Irish army in 1686. Exported 3 Irish regiments to England.
William III and Mary and the Revolution settlement	1697, attacks on William's standing army of foreign soldiers. Huguenot troops sent to Ireland. English parliament demanded the disbanding of all foreign troops and any troops in Ireland over the number of 12,000.	James's Irish regiments disbanded.	In 1689, Tyrconnell raised a Catholic army to support James, supplemented by troops provided by Louis XIV of France; James arrived.

Taxation

Restoration settlement and Charles II	Parliament voted Charles customs and excise, supplemented by Hearth Tax 1662. Increasing percentage of crown revenues from indirect rather than direct taxation.	Taxation regularised. King granted £480,000 per annum for life from customs and excise. Land tax and cess (tax on property) introduced as exceptional measures for military purposes.	King granted customs and external excise in perpetuity.
James II and VII			Granted excise in perpetuity.

Taxation (cont'd)

William III and Mary and the Revolution settlement	Parliament declined to vote William and Mary an income sufficient to rule without parliament. Taxation rose to pay for the wars with France, leading to a financial revolution and the creation of the national debt in 1693.	Parliament experimented with new taxes: poll tax 1693, 1695, 1698; hearth tax 1690; cess at raised level.	In 1689, James's Catholic parliament granted him £20,000 a month for 13 months.

Church

Restoration settlement and Charles II	Bishops and Church of England parish organisation and liturgy restored in 1660. In 1662, all ministers required to take Act of Uniformity; 2,000 ministers (about 10 per cent) declined to be part of the Church of England. Nonconformists persecuted under the terms of the Clarendon Code. In 1662 and 1672, Charles issued Declaration of Indulgence suspending the operation of laws that forbade Catholic or nonconformist worship: both were withdrawn. Test Act 1673 excluded Catholics and Protestant non-conformists from holding elected or civic office.	Bishops restored in 1661, appointed by king. Main administration of church remained with the General Assembly and with the hierarchy of assemblies down to parish level (kirk sessions). 1662 statutes revived lay patronage, declared covenants unlawful, forbade private conventicles. 270 Covenanting ministers (about 25 per cent of the total) refused to accept church settlement in 1663. From 1669, indulgence allowed limited toleration of milder Covenanters. 1670, preaching at conventicles made a capital offence. 1672, 2nd indulgence. 1681, Test Act.	Bishops and Church of Ireland parish organisation and liturgy restored in 1660.
James II and VII	Issued Declarations of Indulgence in 1687 and 1688.	Parliament declined to agree to set aside civil disabilities for Catholics. In 1686, James declared freedom of worship for Catholics and Quakers by prerogative. 1687, Declaration of Indulgence for Catholics, Quakers and Presbyterians.	Church of Ireland remained unmolested but James made no appointments; Catholic bishops allowed to appear in public in clerical dress; Catholic schools and convents established; Church of Ireland revenues used to subsidise Catholic bishops.

| William III and Mary and the Revolution settlement | 400 Anglican clergy (non-jurors) refused to swear oath of allegiance to William and Mary. 1689 Toleration Act permitted freedom of worship to Protestant dissenters but not to Catholics or Unitarians. Only Anglicans could attend university or hold elected or civic offices. | In 1690, William accepted Scottish demands to re-establish Presbyterian church without bishops. Though Presbyterianism was restored, the covenants were not. 152 ministers deprived in 1689 for supporting episcopacy. In 1690, General Assembly met for first time since 1653; from 1694, it regulated its own business and meetings. | Only 1 non-juring Church of Ireland bishop. Church of Ireland in bad state with churches in disrepair and few effective clergy. Presbyterians in Ulster increased by immigrants from Scotland. 1695, 1st of penal laws against Catholics, prohibiting Catholics from education, carrying arms, or owning a horse worth more than £5. In 1697, Catholic bishops and regular clergy banished. Parish clergy had to register under law of 1704. |

SPECIMEN ANSWER

1 During the period 1649–60, Scotland and Ireland had been absorbed into a single British state. But before that and after that neither had been able to operate entirely as sovereign states. Within the three kingdoms, the relationship between monarch, executive and legislature had varied over the period. Neither the Scottish nor the Irish parliament had been able to assume as much control over the monarch as the English parliament had, but the monarch retained a number of important powers:

   • the right to dispense individuals from the law (but not to suspend the laws)
   • the right to summon and dissolve parliament (subject to the Triennial Acts)
   • the right to appoint councillors and judges.

2 By 1691, it was quite clear that the monarch was under the law and that the basis of his/her relationship with his/her subjects was that of contract rather than divine right. One important change that affected the monarch's relations with each of the three nations was the escalating cost of government. Even without warfare, ordinary administration was impossible without grants of taxation from parliament. This inevitably subjected royal policy to greater scrutiny.

In order to take back the throne with minimal bloodshed, Charles II had put aside any hopes he might have had of asserting a claim to divine right to rule, whatever had been the aspirations of his father and grandfather (Charles I and James I and VI) along those lines, and regardless of the potent example of absolutism across the Channel at the court of his cousin, Louis XIV of France. Arbitrary rule had been rejected in the British Isles, first, with the removal of Charles I and, then, with the failure of the Protectorate government. Compromises had to be made in order for Charles II and then William III to take up the throne offered to them, and both had been prepared to make them.

Accepting a more constitutionally nuanced form of rule as the price of the throne did not mean that the later Stuart kings assented willingly to a diminution of their powers. All the monarchs of this period tested the extent of their powers, some with more impunity than others. Even Charles II flouted the Triennial Act and William had an extensive dispute over the maintenance of a standing army in peacetime in defiance of the Bill of Rights. The state in 1691 was not one in which the people had unequivocally triumphed.

REFERENCES

An Account of the Transactions in the North of Ireland, Anno Domini, 1691 (1692) London.

Coward, B. (2003 [1980]) *The Stuart Age: England 1603–1714*, 3rd edn, Harlow, Pearson.

Donaldson, G. (1978 [1965]) *Scotland: James V – James VII*, Edinburgh History of Scotland, vol. 3, Edinburgh, Oliver and Boyd.

Evelyn, J. (n.d.) *Diary* (ed. W. Bray), London, Simpkin, Marshall, Hamilton, Kent & co.

Fyfe, J.G. (ed.) (1928) *Scottish Diaries and Memoirs 1550–1746*, Stirling, Eneas Mackay.

Hutton, R. (1990) *The British Republic 1649–1660*, London, Macmillan.

Russell, C. (2000 [1987]) 'The British problem and the English civil war' in Gaunt, P. (ed.) *The English Civil War*, Oxford, Blackwell, pp. 79–103.

Simms, J.G. (1978a) 'The Restoration 1660–85' in Moody, T.W., Martin, F.X. and Byrne, F.J. (eds) *A New History of Ireland*, vol. 3, *Early Modern Ireland 1534–1691*, Oxford, Clarendon Press, pp. 420–53.

Simms, J.G. (1978b) 'The war of the two kings 1685–91' in Moody, T.W., Martin, F.X. and Byrne, F.J. (eds) *A New History of Ireland*, vol. 3, *Early Modern Ireland 1534–1691*, Oxford, Clarendon Press, pp. 478–508.

Simms, J.G. (1986) 'The establishment of Protestant ascendancy, 1691–1714' in Moody, T.W. and Vaughan, W.E. (eds) *A New History of Ireland*, vol. 4, *Eighteenth-Century Ireland*, Oxford, Clarendon Press, pp. 1–30.

Williams, E.N. (1960) *The Eighteenth-Century Constitution: Documents and Commentary 1688–1815*, Cambridge, Cambridge University Press.

Rachel C. Gibbons and Anne Laurence

CIVIL WARS OR REVOLUTION?

Over recent decades, historians have been divided over the revolutionary nature of the Wars of the Three Kingdoms, and debate on all sides has been passionate. In his article 'Shifting perspectives on the Great Rebellion' that you read in Units 9 and 10, Austin Woolrych concluded that radical elements in the 1650s were marginal and 'there was nothing like the social revolution ... imagined' by the most prominent mid-twentieth century historians, such as the eminent and highly readable Christopher Hill. Although concluding that 'the English revolution ended in a sordid compromise' (quoted in George, 1988, p. 18), Hill insisted that events of the 1640s had dismantled the old 'feudal' order and created a new political structure within which a bourgeois capitalist class could develop. Such a view is not confined to those subscribing to historical materialism (see Unit 9, pp. 11–12): there are other historians who see in the events of the Civil Wars the beginnings of the institutions and values of a modern state and society, even if they do not subscribe to the economic and/or class analysis. During the Commonwealth, a republic was formed briefly, a parliament sat with a much enlarged franchise and power over the head of state, and there was limited religious toleration. But the failure of these reforms and the periodic reversion to the power of the military during the 1650s suggest that there was no group whose interests were really served by such a revolution.

The idea that it was, rather, 1688 and the accession of William and Mary that constituted the real revolution has been associated with what is known as the 'Whig interpretation of history' – a historiographical viewpoint that you encountered in the *Module Companion* and Unit 1. One of its most famous exponents, G.M. Trevelyan (1876–1962), wrote that, while other European states were developing military despotism, England developed a system of government that showed the world 'how liberty could mean not weakness but strength' (Trevelyan, 1949 [1904], p. xii). While neither 1660 nor 1688 created an enlarged franchise – it was necessary to wait until 1832 for that, as you'll see in Block 5 – the Revolution of 1688 formally confirmed that the monarch ruled under the law, not above it, and that law was made in parliament. Under the Act for Establishing the Coronation Oath 1689, the monarch was asked to assent under oath to the question: 'Will you solemnly promise and swear to govern the people of the kingdom of England and the dominions thereunto belonging, *according to the statutes in parliament agreed on, and the laws and customs of the same?*' (emphasis added) (Williams, 1960, p. 37). A direct contrast with the absolute monarchy of Louis XIV's France was celebrated at the time, and has been part of the Whig view of history since, with the sense that gradual steps towards a constitutional monarchy over the seventeenth century spared Britain the violence of the French Revolution – 'these calamities our Revolution averted' (Macaulay, 1906 [1849], p. 210). Few historians now would agree with Macaulay and Trevelyan that the 1688 Revolution was fully progressive, particularly those with an interest in Scottish or Irish history, but the process of political change that it ushered in – the Bill of Rights 1689, the Toleration Act 1689, the Triennial Act 1694 and the Act of Settlement 1701 – certainly secured early steps towards religious toleration, freedom of speech, the supremacy of parliament and restrictions on the powers of the monarch. If you wish, you can see full texts of each of these Acts via the Justis UK Acts website (see Library resources on the A200 website).

THE CIVIL WARS' LEGACY AND THE MODULE THEMES

State formation

A period of regime change and political upheaval is, clearly, one in which the formation of the state was in flux. The exercise that you undertook at the end of Unit 12 (Table 12.4) made clear the gradual evolution of the constitution and the powers of ruler and legislature between the death of Charles I and the end of the seventeenth century, with reforms granted and/or fought for over the course of the Civil Wars within the three kingdoms.

We must also, though, consider the role of external warfare in state building during this period, and beyond. Jonathan Scott concludes that:

> For Charles I war ... was essential to monarchical power. For William [III], monarchical power was essential to war. Accordingly the constitutional changes of 1689–1701, while securing parliaments, also recovered, after a century of disaster, the military substance of English monarchy. This parliamentary monarchy was the centre-piece of the newly constructed English state. It was thus in the context of this military struggle that there occurred all those constitutional alterations which amounted to the creation of a strong parliamentary monarchy.
>
> (Scott, 2000, p. 483)

Scott places the development of the modern British state firmly in the context of European war. William's accession in 1688, and French support of James II, propelled the kingdoms of the British Isles alongside the Dutch into the League of Augsburg (the Grand Alliance) and war against Louis XIV's France (1689–97). William needed the support of parliament and the taxation only it could raise in order successfully to pursue this foreign policy. The enormity of the impact of the Civil Wars and the constitutional settlements of 1660 and 1688–89 rightly absorb the attention of historians of this period. However, it is important that, in concentrating on developments internal to the British Isles, we do not neglect the wider and longer-term ramifications of those developments. The 1688 Revolution did more than replace one king with another. The 'Anglo-Dutch collaboration' (Scott, 2000, p. 16) of parliament and William III rejected the French-sympathising position of James II/VII and, instead, saw France's power as a threat within Europe and a rival overseas in

Asian, North American and Caribbean colonies. The European context is important to state formation and the consequences of the Civil Wars, as well as to their origins and beliefs and ideologies.

Beliefs and ideologies

In Unit 10 (pp. 33–4), we saw that many historians accord religion a prominent place in the Civil Wars. John Morrill argues that they were not the first European revolution, but the 'last of the [European] Wars of Religion'. He takes the view that discontent with Charles I in the three kingdoms:

> lacked the momentum, the passion, to bring about the kind of civil war ... experienced in 1642. It was the force of religion that drove minorities to fight, and forced majorities to make reluctant choices.
>
> (Morrill, 1993 [1984], p. 47)

Scott makes a slightly different connection with the wider picture of the wars of religion:

> The crisis of 1618–48 threw not only the whole of religiously mixed, half-reformed central and western Europe into conflict, but Britain too, because Britain was part of religiously mixed, half-reformed central and western Europe.
>
> (Scott, 2000, p. 28)

EXERCISE

From your knowledge of Scott and Morrill's arguments from Unit 10 (pp. 33–4) and material in this Conclusion so far, how would you characterise differences of approach and views between these two historians?

Spend about 10 minutes on this exercise.

SPECIMEN ANSWER

Scott sees the British Isles as part of a wider European pattern, resembling other European states in the significance of warfare for state building and also in the variable spread of reformed beliefs in states classing themselves as Protestant or Catholic. Morrill, by contrast, regards continental Europe's experience as offering a basis for comparison, but believes that it was essentially internal differences within the established Protestant churches that drove people to civil war in the British Isles.

DISCUSSION

Both historians are concerned with the nature of the state and with its relation to religious beliefs and ideologies. Both also see the role of religion in the seventeenth century as, to some extent, unfinished business. Morrill largely looks backwards, seeing the Wars of the Three Kingdoms as primarily a conflict over religion and the last of a sequence of events of the Protestant Reformations and the Counter-Reformation. Scott is more concerned with looking forwards, arguing that the constitutional outcome of the Civil Wars, in the post-1688 settlement, was a necessary precondition for the eventual British state.

We could argue that both are right, in that struggles between Protestants over the extent and direction of reform within the established national churches were so prominent in the origins of the wars in Scotland and England. Equally, the deposition of James II and acceptance of William III and Mary II in 1688 indicated that, whatever else the political classes in England demanded of their monarch, chief was that he or she had to be an Anglican. The Bill of Rights of 1689 states that 'it hath been found by experience that it is inconsistent with the safety of this protestant kingdom to be governed by a popish prince' (Williams, 1960, p. 32). The Coronation Act 1689 mandated future monarchs to swear to 'maintain the laws of God, the true profession of the Gospel and the protestant reformed religion established by law' (Williams, 1960, p. 37). Opposition to the Glorious Revolution and support for James was driven as much by religious affiliation as political loyalties among Catholic Irish while, in Scotland, when Presbyterianism was established as the national church in 1690 and bishops were abolished, those who left the church because they believed in the episcopacy lived uneasily with the accusation that they were also Jacobites and, thereby, potential traitors.

Producers and consumers

We saw in Unit 11 something of the effects of the Civil Wars on local manufacturing, industry and consumption, while the impact of taxation and financial impositions from king and parliament also featured in Units 10 and 11. Over the course of the seventeenth century, foreign trade also became of increasing importance. The separate nations of the British Isles did not share a customs union, so there were customs dues to pay on goods transported between England (with Wales), on the one hand, and Scotland and Ireland. England was larger, richer and more populous, had better developed industry and agriculture, and a succession of Acts after the Restoration of Charles II gave England control of most British international trade. The Navigation Act 1660 and the Irish Cattle Acts of 1663 and 1667 inhibited the trade of Scotland and Ireland to protect that of England, for example.

The most important changes in the economy took place under William III, and were direct consequences of his wars with France. The foundation of the Bank of England and creation of the national debt facilitated the war and enabled the building up of the navy, not only as the country's chief defence but, also, as an instrument of commercial policy. These changes, in turn, would lead to the financial revolution that created the stock market and modern banking, facilitating global change, as you will learn in Block 6. The Nine Years War (1689–97) against Louis XIV was not restricted only to Europe but drew in English, Dutch and French colonies in North America, the Caribbean, India and south-east Asia, establishing a pattern for wars between European powers in the eighteenth and nineteenth centuries (Blocks 4 and 6).

REFERENCES

George, C.H. (1988) 'Christopher Hill: a profile' in Eley, G. and Hunt, W. (eds) *Reviving the English Revolution: Reflections and Elaborations on the Work of Christopher Hill*, London, Verso.

Macaulay, T.B. (1906 [1849]) *History of England from the Accession of James II*, vol. 1, London, Everyman.

Morrill, J. (1993 [1984]) 'The religious context of the English civil war' in *The Nature of the English Revolution*, London, Longman, pp. 45–68.

Scott, J. (2000) *England's Troubles: Seventeenth-Century English Political Instability in a European Context*, Cambridge, Cambridge University Press.

Trevelyan, G.M. (1949 [1904]) *England under the Stuarts*, 29th edn, London, Methuen.

Williams, E.N. (1960) *The Eighteenth-Century Constitution: Documents and Commentary, 1688–1815*, Cambridge, Cambridge University Press.

FURTHER READING

Barnard, T. (2004) *The Kingdom of Ireland, 1641–1760*, Basingstoke, Palgrave Macmillan.

Braddick, M. (2009) *God's Fury, England's Fire: A New History of the English Civil Wars*, Harmondsworth, Penguin.

Macinnes, A. (2005) *The British Revolution 1629–1660*, Basingstoke, Palgrave Macmillan.

Royle, T. (2005 [2004]) *The Civil War: The War of the Three Kingdoms, 1638–1660*, new edn, London, Abacus.

Smith, D.L. (1998) *A History of the Modern British Isles 1603–1707: The Double Crown*, Oxford, Blackwell.

GLOSSARY

agitators: representatives elected in 1647 to press the grievances of soldiers in the New Model regiments.

Anglican: of the **Church of England** or **Church of Ireland**. Both churches were headed by the monarch and governed by bishops, and both followed the services specified in the Book of Common Prayer and theology set out in the Thirty-Nine Articles.

apostolic succession: belief that bishops were the direct spiritual descendants of Christ's apostles, through the ceremony of the laying on of hands.

Arminian: supporter of the beliefs published by Jacob Arminius that grace (salvation) could be earned; beliefs favoured by those who rejected the doctrine of predestination.

assessment: weekly tax.

canons: regulations governing the **Church of England** and the **Church of Ireland**.

Church of England: Protestant church founded as a consequence of Henry VIII's breach with the papacy in the 1530s. Its secular head was the monarch, its ecclesiastical head was the archbishop of Canterbury and it was administered by bishops. Until 1689, attendance at its services was enforced by law.

Church of Ireland: Protestant church founded in 1540 after Henry VIII's breach with the papacy in the 1530s. Its secular head was the monarch, its ecclesiastical head was the archbishop of Armagh and it was administered by bishops. Doctrinally similar to the **Church of England**, but not identical.

Church of Scotland: Protestant church founded in 1560, often called the **Kirk**. Its organisation was Presbyterian (by assemblies) and its theology was Calvinist.

Commonwealth: often used by historians to describe the parliament-led regimes of 1649–53 and 1659–60 (thus excluding years of the **Protectorate** (1653–9)). Legally, though, the whole period of the **Interregnum**, between the execution of the king (1649) and the Restoration, was a Commonwealth, which is how the term is used in this block.

communion: see **Holy Communion**.

Confederate: of the Irish Catholic **Confederation of Kilkenny**.

Confederation of Kilkenny: alliance of Gaelic Irish and Old English who established a Catholic provisional government in Kilkenny from 1642 to 1649.

conventicle: illegal religious congregation.

convention: an assembly resembling parliament but not called by the monarch (called in 1660 and 1688).

Covenant: see **Solemn League and Covenant** and **National Covenant**.

Covenanter: supporter of the Scottish **National Covenant**.

debenture: document guaranteeing the right to an allocation of land in lieu of pay; most commonly used of the scheme to allocate Irish land to pay Cromwellian forces there.

deposition: sworn statement.

dissenter: one who dissented from the **Church of England**'s **liturgy** and worship; normally used of only Protestants after 1660.

divine right of kings: belief that the king owed his powers to God and was answerable to God for the protection of his subjects.

Engagement: alliance between the king and the Scots made in 1647.

Engager: supporter of Charles I's '**Engagement**' with the Covenanting Scots.

episcopate: body of bishops.

Eucharist: see **Holy Communion**.

free grace: doctrine that salvation is not foreordained but given freely by God.

Gaelic Irish: native Irish, Gaelic-speaking Catholics who retained in the seventeenth century some vestiges of their earlier clan organisation.

General Assembly of the Kirk: see **Kirk, General Assembly of the**.

Holy Communion: bread and the wine administered at a communion service to the laity by the minister (Protestant) or the bread administered at the Mass to the laity by the priest, the wine was taken only by the priest (Roman Catholic). Also known as the Eucharist.

Homilies, Book of: collection of written addresses used by **Anglican** clergy who could not preach their own sermons.

Humble Petition and Advice: revised Protectorate constitution of 1657.

Independent: one who believed in a church based on a voluntary gathered congregation, each being self-sufficient with no organisation beyond the individual congregation.

Instrument of Government: constitution establishing the Protectorate in 1653.

Interregnum: interval between kings, usually used of the period 1649–60.

Jacobite: supporter of the deposed James II and VII, and/or of his son the Old Pretender.

Kirk: see **Church of Scotland**.

Kirk, General Assembly of the: national governing body of the **Church of Scotland** with both clerical and lay members.

kirk session: group of elders (presbyters) elected by each local church community as a governing body; the meeting attended by presbyters. Groups of local churches were governed by a higher assembly of elders (a **presbytery**), and these regional presbyteries fed into the meetings of the **General Assembly of the Kirk**.

liturgy: order of service; **Anglican** liturgy published in Book of Common Prayer.

minister (of the church): functionary appointed either by a bishop (**Anglican**) or by a congregation (**nonconformist**) to conduct services and minister to the faithful.

mortality crisis: exceptionally raised death rate.

National Covenant: a document stating that changes to the **Church of Scotland** required the approval of the **General Assembly of the Kirk** and parliament, and could not be decreed by the king. In February 1638, it was subscribed in Edinburgh and circulated to every burgh and parish for signature.

New English: Protestant Englishmen and women who settled in Ireland from the sixteenth century on.

nonconformist: one who did not conform to the **Anglican** Church's **liturgy** and worship; normally a Protestant.

Old English: descendants of the twelfth-century Norman invaders of Ireland; predominantly Catholic, though some Protestant converts. They dominated the government of Ireland until the mid seventeenth century. Many spoke Irish (Gaelic) and had married into Gaelic Irish families.

planter: settler on an allocation of land; usually used of the English and Scots who took up allocations of land confiscated from rebellious Catholic Irish landowners.

predestinarian: one who believes in predestination.

prelacy: system of church government by bishops.

prerogative: particular power reserved to monarch.

Presbyterian: believer in a system of church government by a hierarchy of assemblies (**presbyteries**) with lay and clerical members. Often associated with Calvinist doctrine.

presbytery: assembly of lay people and ministers from several parishes charged with administering those parishes.

priest: Roman Catholic clergyman; used as a term of abuse of ceremonialist Protestant clergy.

Protectorate: government under the lords protector, Oliver Cromwell (1653–58) and his son Richard (1658–59).

Protestor: see **Remonstrant (or Protestor)**.

Puritan: someone who believed that the reform of the **Anglican** Church had not gone far enough in a Protestant direction; usually used before 1660.

regicide: act of killing a king; one of those who signed King Charles I's death warrant.

Remonstrant (or Protestor): supporter of the Remonstrance (October 1650), which denounced any understanding with Charles II and sought to enforce the Act of Classes.

Resolutioner: supporter of alliance between moderate **Covenanters** and royalists.

Solemn League and Covenant: both the military alliance of 1643 between Scotland and England, and the agreement that the English would implement the Scottish system of church government; signed by members of parliament and the parliamentary army.

subsidy: direct tax granted to the king by parliament to meet particular occasions.

tonnage and poundage: tax on imports granted to the king at his accession by parliament.

Westminster Assembly of Divines: assembly established in 1643 to devise a new church settlement for England and Wales in accordance with the terms of the **Solemn League and Covenant**.

INDEX